AF573618

The Beginnings at Whatcombe

By the same Author

The Liturgy of Penance

The Feast of Pentecost

Christmas and Epiphany

Commentary on the New Lectionary

Greater Things than These: a Personal Account of the Charismatic Movement

The Charismatic Prayer Group: A Handbook for Leaders, Members and Clergy

The Beginnings at Whatcombe

AN EXPERIENCE OF COMMUNITY

by

JOHN GUNSTONE

Drawings by Sylvia Lawton

HODDER AND STOUGHTON
LONDON SYDNEY AUCKLAND TORONTO

To

MOLEY and LIONEL,

and to NAN,

for their love, their prayers, and

their encouragement

Copyright © 1976 by John Gunstone. *First printed 1976. ISBN 0 340 20994 1.* *All rights reserved. No part of this publication may be reproduced or transmitted in any form or by any means, electronic or mechanical, including photocopy, recording, or any information storage and retrieval systems, without permission in writing from the publisher. This book is sold subject to the condition that it shall not, by way of trade or otherwise, be lent, resold, hired out or otherwise circulated without the publisher's prior consent in any form of binding or cover other than that in which this is published and without a similar condition including this condition being imposed on the subsequent purchaser.* *Printed in Great Britain for Hodder and Stoughton Limited, London by Cox & Wyman Ltd., London, Reading and Fakenham.*

Foreword

by

REG EAST

Warden of the Barnabas Fellowship, Whatcombe House

FOR THOSE OF US involved in the birth and development of the Barnabas Fellowship, it has been an experience for which we are grateful to God. It may well be that we are in the early stages of its life, since it has been in existence only four and a half years. But already the effect of God's hand upon us is evident, and so some account of its life may not be premature.

What the Barnabas Fellowship has to offer which is peculiarly its own is its community life. The teaching, the ministry and the care of our guests can be paralleled by communities and groups all through the Church, but our community life is unique because a particular set of people form it. What we have to give is, what God has been able to do with us and what we have become since being here.

Living in community has had a profound effect on us all. Nothing has challenged us more, no previous experience has demanded more change. The fact that we still exist as a community is a tribute solely to the grace of God. He alone — in ways which we find difficult to pinpoint — has welded a motley group of strong-minded people into a unity of love. There has been misunderstanding, self-pity, anger and suffering, but gloriously the Holy Spirit has broken through our differing backgrounds, churchmanships, prejudices and sins, to bring us to repentance and acceptance of each other.

For our part, a conviction that we had been called by God to this life and a determination to learn to love, have been the response to God's grace which we were able to make. For most of the time this has been a small enough response, yet from such a meagre offering the love of Christ has somehow filtered through to bring peace among us.

It was to this that we were called. Years before we were formed, the Holy Spirit spoke in prophecy (in the prayer group at Mersea described on p. 14) saying that the future house was to be "a house of peace and of prayer". We have tried to make prayer pervade our common life, and others say they feel the peace. In another prophecy our Lord said, "As I your God am Three in love, so there are three things that you must have — love, obedience and faith. These are three sisters walking hand in hand . . . and these are the three keys that open all doors . . . You will be the key I handle, the key I take in my hand to open and undo the locks that bind my suffering children." This has been one of our greatest privileges — to enter into and share the pain and grief of so many, and be used for their release into freedom and joy.

No account of our life can adequately express these things, but it may well be that John's story will encourage others to step out in faith as Christ calls at this time of great opportunity.

Introduction

RECENT YEARS HAVE seen the springing up of many small Christian communities. Some of these have been formed when individuals have experienced personal renewal in the Holy Spirit through what is called the charismatic movement. More aware of the unifying grace of Jesus Christ in their lives, they have been drawn together by God into a closer fellowship. The Barnabas Fellowship is one of these communities.

It was my privilege to be a member of it for the first four years of its life at Whatcombe House in Dorset. This book is an account of my experiences. In it I have tried to describe how from the beginning we faced together the problems of communal living, how I saw the Lord working through those around me in the community, and how we learned the joys and strengths of a corporate ministry in the Body of Christ.

As in much else that I undertook during those four years, the members encouraged me while this book was being written and read the manuscript in its final stages before it was completed. I must stress, however, that they are not responsible for what I have said. This book is about my observation of and reaction to community life. Each other member of the Fellowship could tell of other observations and different reactions. But we are one in a deep thankfulness to God for all that he has done for us by bringing us together for this adventure in discipleship.

I went to Whatcombe in 1971 with the idea of staying for about a year. It used to be said that clergymen who had done twenty years' parochial work ought to have a sabbatical, and I regarded the invitation to join the community as an opportunity for just that. (I had been a parish priest in the Church of England for nineteen years.)

But, as the months went by, I found myself more and more involved in a ministry of teaching about renewal in the Spirit from a vantage-point where I could see the Lord renewing so much of his Church. Also, in the community I experienced a loving relationship with fellow-Christians such as I had rarely experienced before. So, instead of staying at Whatcombe for one year, I remained for four.

One further point. I have told the story of these four years in the past tense. For me they are a part of my personal history. But I ask readers to remember that the Barnabas Fellowship is still very active. Those years are only the beginning of a continuing story as its members fulfil the ministry to which God has called them in his Church. He does great things in them and through them today: whereof we rejoice.

JOHN GUNSTONE

All Saints' Day, 1975.

I

Reg East and I were ordained in the diocese of Chelmsford in the early 'fifties. While I was serving in a second curacy, he was the bishop's chaplain for youth, and for several summers I helped at the holiday conferences which he and his wife, Lucia, organised in St. Monica's School, Clacton-on-Sea.

These conferences gave all three of us insights into what the Lord can do when a group of his people live, pray and work together. Through the fellowship at St. Monica's, and especially through the worship, we saw many young people brought to a deeper love for Jesus Christ. It was at Clacton that Reg and Lucia discovered the gift they have for helping people to feel quickly at home in a conference situation.

Reg and I became incumbents in the diocese at about the same time. He was appointed vicar of East and West Mersea near Colchester; I went to St. Augustine's Church, Rush Green, Romford, at the other end of Essex in what is known as London-over-the-Border. We visited one another several times a year, sharing in the problems, joys and hopes of parish life. Reg and Lucia invited me to be the godfather of their younger daughter, Catherine.

We had been incumbents for about five years when the charismatic movement, the "new pentecostalism", began to touch Christians in England. Reg and Lucia had been sent magazines and books on the renewal in the Spirit that was being experienced by Christians in the Episcopalian and other established Churches in the U.S.A. Reg received the laying on of hands and was "baptised in the Spirit" early in 1963; his wife had the same experience a few days later.

I knew that something very profound was happening in their lives and I asked them to tell me about it. After meeting other people who had been baptised in the Spirit, I asked Reg to pray for me. This he did with the laying on of hands. About a week later, when I was praying alone in my church in Rush Green, I had an overwhelming awareness of the presence of Almighty God and I discovered that I was able to praise him with the gift of tongues. I attended some of the prayer meetings which Reg organised in Mersea vicarage, and it was there that I was introduced to the characteristically "charismatic" ways of corporate prayer and ministry.*

Among other things, Reg's experience had the effect of bringing into sharper focus an idea that he had had for several years. It was that one day God would lead him out of parochial work to establish a small community to staff a conference centre. The origins of this idea are to be found partly in his work as youth chaplain at Clacton and partly

* I have described these experiences in more detail in the first chapter of *Greater Things than These* (Faith Press, 1974.)

in the association which he had with Lee Abbey in Devon. During early morning prayer one day in 1966 he had a picture of about a dozen Christians serving thirty or forty guests in a large house. He had no doubts that this picture had been given to him by the Lord.

One day he told me about it.

I can remember now the strange feeling of warm enthusiasm that came over me as I listened to him, and when he had finished I blurted out: 'Reg, I'd like to come in with you!"

A few minutes later Lucia walked into the room.

"John says he'd like to come in with us if we form a community," Reg told her.

Lucia looked at me wryly.

"Do you think you could stand our children?" she asked.

The answer seemed to be put into my mouth: "They'll be older then."

I have never uttered a more exact prophecy.

It must have been at about this time that two married couples who were members of St. Clement's Church, Openshaw, Manchester, were baptised in the Spirit and organised a weekly prayer meeting in their homes. Ron Dodgson and Ken Taylor were licensed readers at the church. Ron's wife, Jean, and Ken's wife, Betty, were much involved in the activities of the congregation. Ron and Jean had believed for several years that they would be led out into full-time Christian work, but they had no indication of what form this would take.

Later in 1966 Ron and Jean booked to go to a Fountain Trust conference on renewal at High Leigh near Hoddesdon.

Reg and Lucia had been invited by Michael Harper, Director of the Fountain Trust, to act as host and hostess at that conference. A fortnight before the conference, during a prayer meeting in Mersea, they had been given a prophecy — through an interpretation following a gift of tongues — that at High Leigh they would meet a couple who would join them in forming the community they had thought and prayed about for so long. They drove to High Leigh with this prophecy lifting their hopes.

At the conference Reg and Lucia met the two from Manchester briefly on the first day but did not speak to them again for the rest of the week — there were over two hundred people at High Leigh. The Easts were so busy that they forgot about the prophecy.

On the last day Ron and Jean were in their car driving away from the conference centre when Jean said, "I think the Lord wants us to go back and speak to Reg."

"I think so too," said Ron.

He turned the car round and went back up the drive.

Ron and Jean found Reg in the entrance hall clearing away some papers. Feeling slightly awkward, they went up to him. "We've come back — er — to say goodbye to you," they said.

Reg remembered the prophecy as he looked at them. Was this the couple? . . .

He took them to a room, asked them to wait, and went in search of Lucia. He told her that a man and his wife had come back to speak to him and that he felt they should be told about the incident in the Mersea prayer meeting. She agreed.

About half-an-hour later the Dodgsons were in their car once more on the road to Manchester.

"Me — in a community?" exclaimed Jean, thinking of the house they were buying on a mortgage. "Never!"

Yet, in spite of these misgivings, the Easts and the Dodgsons exchanged letters and visited one another to discuss the project and to pray about it. Slowly the conviction grew that the Lord had brought them together for this purpose, and they began to inspect properties in various parts of England when an opportunity presented itself. They saw disused convents, empty country houses, and even one or two schools, but nothing fitted in with Reg's picture of a place that could accommodate a small community and thirty to forty guests. In the late 'sixties it began to be a poor joke in our conversation.

"Well," I used to say when I saw Reg and Lucia "have you found anywhere yet?"

"No," they would reply resignedly, and attempt to look hopeful about it.

A visit to the Mary Sisterhood at Darmstadt had a profound effect on the Easts. There they experienced a quality of penitence that was a revelation to them. They learned how the Holy Spirit brought to Christians a deeper contrition for human disobedience as well as a greater joy for God's love, and how the charismatic movement touches all aspects of Christian thinking and devotion.

Something else happened at Darmstadt that they were to remember with gratitude.

One day Lucia noticed that an American guest was wearing an attractive little silver cross with the figure of a dove embossed upon it — a symbol of Christ's death and resurrection and of the gift of the Spirit.

"That's lovely," she cried.

The wearer allowed Lucia to handle it.

Next day, the American came back to her.

"I feel the Lord wants me to give you this," she said, handing Lucia the little silver cross.

Embarrassed, Lucia tried to return the gift, but the donor refused. Years later that cross became the emblem of the Barnabas Fellowship.

* * *

In January, 1971, Michael Harper heard that a large house was available for rent in Dorset and, knowing that Reg and Lucia were looking for a place in which they could live in community, he passed the news on to Mersea Vicarage.

The message reached Reg whilst he was in the middle of a post-Christmas rush of parish work. He nearly ignored it, but looking at his diary he saw there was one free day at the end of the month when he and Lucia could, if they started early in the morning, drive down to Dorset and back.

This they did. Leaving Mersea soon after midnight, they drove across southern England in wintry weather, stopping for breakfast at a restaurant near Blandford, and arrived at the house at ten o'clock in the morning.

In the January light and chilly drizzle Whatcombe was anything but inviting. Built in the middle of the eighteenth century and extensively altered at the beginning of the nineteenth, it looked like a huge box dumped on the slope of a gentle hill among scattered clumps of old trees. The walls of the house have been rendered with grey-coloured concrete, etched to give the impression of stonework, and this gives the place a sombre look, even in sunlight. But the house has a simple grandeur. Coupled Ionic pilasters rise beside the main doorway, which is in the centre of the east façade, and over the doors is a coat-of-arms in a lunette.

Three fine windows on either side of this doorway are matched by similar windows on the first and second floors, and in the centre of the first floor is a Palladian window.

Reg and Lucia wandered from room to room, a feeling of hope alternating with a sense of despair. The main building, with its fine lounge and library, was in a good condition, but the extensions at the back were in a poor state.

it was obvious that many months' work would be needed before that part of the house could be lived in.

Until the Second World War the house had been the home of the Pleydell-Railston family. After that, it had been let to various groups, but it had been empty for two years (except for a caretaker) when Reg and Lucia saw it. Mrs. Pleydell-Railston lived in a more modern house about half-a-mile from Whatcombe, and Whatcombe itself belonged to one of her daughters, Mrs. Patricia Chichester.

A few weeks later Reg and Lucia visited Whatcombe again with Ron and Jean. Ron's engineering background enabled him to see that, although much needed to be done, most of it was not beyond the scope of a team of people willing to tackle the job on a do-it-yourself basis. The decision was taken to discuss with Mrs. Chichester's agent the possibility of renting the house. While the four of them prayed about the decision before returning to their respective homes in Mersea and Manchester, the figure of one thousand pounds a year came into their minds.

The Easts met the agent in London.

"The rent paid by the previous tenants has been quite uneconomic," he told them. (Their hearts sank!) "We feel that we must raise it considerably."

"How much?" they asked.

"How does the figure of eight hundred pounds appear to you?"

"And the rates?"

"About two hundred pounds a year."

They could hardly believe their ears! The two sums added up to the total they had been given whilst they prayed with Ron and Jean. But their delight disappeared with the agent's next remark. A guarantee of five years' rent would be required before they could use the house, plus a further five thousand pounds' deposit in the bank as additional security. It was, the agent pointed out, for their benefit that the projected conference centre should have a strong financial basis.

Ten thousand pounds! That sounded an enormous figure to a vicar and his wife who had little personal savings. It looked as if God, having slightly opened a door, was slamming it shut again!

Yet they continued to plan—and pray. If it was the Lord's will that they should go to Whatcombe to found a new community, then he would provide the necessary cash without a public appeal.

Both the Easts and the Dodgsons now began to receive gifts of money and offers of interest-free loans. In Mersea an elderly member of Reg's congregation sold her house when she moved into an old people's home and gave him three thousand pounds from the proceeds. Another donated a thousand pounds. A former school-teacher put an envelope containing five hundred pounds through the vicarage door with a note saying that he had intended leaving Reg this amount in his will but had since decided to give it to him in person! Members of the prayer meeting which Ron, Jean, Ken and Betty organised in Manchester also gave sums of money.

By Easter the Easts and the Dodgsons agreed that they would leave their homes and their jobs that summer and begin to live at Whatcombe as a community.

During the Easter holidays Reg and Lucia took their three children, Elizabeth, Mark and Catherine, to Lucia's parents at Swanage. Lionel and "Moley" Osborn had not been told anything about Whatcombe. Lucia had not wished to burden them with the idea of what might seem to them a risky undertaking. But now that the decision had been made, Lionel and Moley had to be informed.

Moley listened with mixed feelings. On the one hand she was thrilled that her daughter's family would be living nearby (Whatcombe is about twenty miles from Swanage); on the other hand she dreaded the thought that the community and the conference centre might not be a success. If it failed, her son-in-law would be without a job and her daughter and grandchildren without a home!

Reg and Lucia urged her to trust in what God was doing. Just before they had left Mersea for Swanage they had been given a gift of five hundred pounds. Wasn't that sufficient to indicate that the community was the Lord's will for them?

That night, after lying awake worrying about the project, Moley got up out of bed and went into the little room which she called her "muckery" to pray. She asked God for a sign. If it was his will that the East family should move to Whatcombe, she said, let him double that five hundred pounds by the end of the week. She crept back to bed wondering if she had done the right thing. She had never asked for a sign before. Next morning she said nothing about it to Reg and Lucia: she thought they might accuse her of lack of faith!

At the end of the holiday the East family drove back to Mersea. When they entered the vicarage, Lucia phoned her mother in Swanage to tell her that they had arrived home safely while Reg opened the letters which had been delivered during their absence. Lucia was still speaking to Moley when Reg held out one letter for her to see.

Attached to it was a cheque for five hundred pounds.

Lucia's gasp of delight was heard by her mother in Swanage.

"What is it?" Moley asked.

"We've just had another gift of five hundred pounds!"

* * *

The next few weeks were frantically busy for Reg, Lucia, Ron and Jean. Reg had to investigate the legal requirements of setting up a trust and to invite people to join the community. Ron and Jean had to sell their house. Jobs had to be given up.

David and Alma Pinkney, friends of the Easts, agreed to act as trustees. David was the director of a firm and his business experience was valuable. Lucia's father, Lionel, also became a trustee, and so did her brother-in-law, John Turner, an estate manager.

Following up my remark eight years previously, Reg invited me to join him at Whatcombe.

The invitation came at an awkward moment. I had been asked to consider taking up another post in the diocese and, although it had not been definitely offered to me, I did not feel sure what the Lord's will for me was. I decided to wait. As the weeks went by, I assisted Reg in a few administrative matters and sketched an article on the new community for the summer number of the Fountain Trust's magazine, *Renewal*.

A few days before I was due to go down to Mersea to

finish the article, I was informed that it would not be possible to offer me the post that had been suggested in the diocese.

Was this the Lord's way of sending me to Whatcombe? I wondered.

The answer came while I was at Mersea. I spent the afternoon sitting in the bay window of the lounge in the vicarage, typing the final version of the article for *Renewal* with the sun streaming down on my papers. When I put the final dot at the end of the last paragraph, it seemed as if the Lord said to me, "Yes, you're to go with them."

I took the completed manuscript into the study for Reg to read.

"By the way," I said, as I handed it to him, "I'd like to accept your offer and come to Whatcombe with you."

2

REG AND LUCIA moved into Whatcombe with their family on 2nd July, 1971. Ron and Jean arrived the same day with their son, Jeffrey, who was a student at a college of education in Manchester. In August they were joined by Ray Lambie, a friend of the Dodgsons; he was a ship's cook who came to Whatcombe for a fortnight's holiday but who stayed as a member of the community for two years! Rosemary Ewens, a young school-teacher whose home was in Mersea, joined a week or two later. I came to Whatcombe on 19th September. The following month we were joined by David and Alma Pinkney, David having left his firm when it was taken over in a merger. The nine of us made up the original members of the community.

When the Easts and the Dodgsons arrived at Whatcombe, they settled themselves temporarily in the rooms on the first floor of the house and took stock. The first problem they had to solve was the allocation of rooms — what part of the house to use for the community and what part for the guests.

The various extensions to Whatcombe over the years

have resulted in a confusing maze of corridors and staircases within the house itself. The entrance hall is in the middle of the east side of the building. When the visitor enters this hall through the main doors, he finds rooms opening off on either side. On his right is the lounge, a spacious room with high windows looking out over the fields and trees; on his left is the library, the same size as the lounge and with a beautifully decorated ceiling and chandelier.

Passing through the entrance hall the visitor enters a second, inner hall. To the right the staircase sweeps upwards with a wrought iron balustrade to the first-floor landing; on the left are two more doors, one to the dining-room on the south side of the house, the other to the passages that lead to the kitchens, pantries, washing-up room ("the dishery") and the rear parts of the building.

There are two more staircases. The first takes the visitor up to the first and second floors and to the north-west wing; the second takes him to the first floor of the extensions at the back.

At first Reg, Lucia, Ron and Jean considered using the rear of the house for the community and the main building for the guests. In the end they decided to use the top floor of the main building and the north-west wing for the community and the rest of the house for the guests. With some alterations, this would leave nineteen guest rooms and rooms for ten or so members of the community.

The married members were to have a sitting-room and a bedroom; the unmarried members a bed-sitter. On the top floor of the main building were the rooms for the East family, Rosemary, Ron and Jean, and myself. The Pinkneys, Ray and Jeffrey were allocated rooms in the north-west wing. The cleaning, repairing and decorating of these rooms began in August and they were nearly ready by the time I arrived in September. From that date we began the massive operation of preparing the rest of the house.

One particular week in September will always stand out in my memory. It was when six people from Manchester stayed with us for a working holiday — members of the prayer group I mentioned in the last chapter. The men sawed and hammered, sang hymns and cracked jokes; the women busied themselves round the house and gardens under the direction of Lucia and Jean. Among them was Ken Taylor. With his wife, Betty, and his youngest son, Jonathan, he had already spent three days at Whatcombe the previous month. The Taylors had been feeling that the Lord was calling them to join the community, but the opportunity to do so did not present itself until the following year.

Three rooms at the back of the house were divided to make extra bedrooms. An additional bedroom and bathroom was created by walling off an open space. Another room was partitioned to provide an extra bathroom. We calculated that by the time we had finished we would have three rooms with four beds, one with three beds, eleven with twin beds and four with single beds — sleeping accommodation for thirty-seven guests, with space for children's beds in the larger rooms.

Although we had enough money in the bank to pay our rent for five years, we did not dare to draw too heavily on our reserves and we had to plan the alterations and decorations as economically as possible. A lot of timber came from discarded furniture found in the basement. Some of the rooms had hardboard nailed to the floors and this was carefully lifted for use on the new walls. Local timber-yards were searched for second-hand wood.

All through the autumn we concentrated on the back of the house where the greatest amount of work had to be done. Ron and I did most of the initial construction and repair. Ron was in charge of this operation, I acted as his mate. We laboured in the midst of the smell of sawdust and the whine of power-tools. I became quite adept at dismantling window-frames and fitting hardboard to new walls.

After us came Reg with sandpaper and Polyfilla, preparing the rooms and corridors for decorating. He was followed by Lucia and Rosemary who painted and papered. Lucia's eye for colour gave the rooms a striking finish. Rosemary who, when she arrived at Whatcombe, had been scared even to put one foot on a ladder, learned how to walk a plank high off the floor, to emulsion a ceiling.

Jean was responsible for the furnishing of each room. Before she left Manchester, she had been able to purchase four hundred yards of curtaining material at the staggeringly cheap price of twenty-five and fifty pence a yard. She set up her sewing machine in one of the large bedrooms and her skill as a tailoress was employed in making curtains. The men moved carpets, beds, dressing-tables and wardrobes under her direction.

Mrs. Chichester employed an electrician and the community engaged a plumber, to do the major work of rewiring the house and installing baths, washbasins and toilets. David did much of the detailed electrical work, making a Tannoy system throughout the house out of old speakers and ends of tins and fitting up an emergency lighting circuit powered from car batteries. His wife, Alma, was in the office, opening letters and answering telephone calls. Ray took time off from the kitchen to tackle the garden.

When we met for prayer each morning we offered our plans for the day and our immediate needs to God. We experienced remarkable answers to our intercessions.

The most obvious need was money. We had no income whatever and we depended entirely on gifts. Cheques came through the post, often in the nick of time to pay a bill or to buy an item of equipment that we urgently required. A friend gave £300 to cover the cost of feeding us during the first three months. Two articles about Whatcombe in the *Church Times* at the beginning of 1972 brought in over two hundred letters, many of them containing cheques or postal orders. Rather shyly we put a small collecting box in our entrance hall, half-hoping casual visitors would notice it, half-hoping they wouldn't!

One caller was a Church Commissioner. Part of his responsibility was to advise on the spending of tens of thousands of pounds each year on the Church's new projects for ministry in England. When he said goodbye he told me he had been amazed at what had been achieved at Whatcombe without any help from official ecclesiastical sources.

* * *

The tale of the carpet has become a minor legend.

The lounge at Whatcombe is too large for any carpet

from an ordinary house. As it happened, the carpets from the Easts' and the Dodgsons' homes were the same pattern and, put side by side, they did not look too bad — to masculine eyes, that is! To feminine eyes they looked terrible. Consequently, the women in the community said they couldn't think of opening the house without new carpets for the lounge and main staircase. The men demurred. I had a long discussion with Jean about the need for holy poverty and the dangers of unnecessary ostentation! The following morning, during our prayers, she asked the Lord to supply us with new carpets. I so disagreed with the request that I did not say "Amen" to her petition!

It so happened that we already had one hundred pounds — a gift from the Fountain Trust. About this time, unknown to us, a friend of the community had been left a legacy. She decided to give us a hundred pounds out of it towards kitchen equipment but, before she delivered the cheque, she was prompted to write the words, "For a Carpet", on the envelope containing it. The next day David and Alma added a further hundred, making three hundred pounds in all.

Then Jean remembered that friends of hers in Manchester had met a Christian carpet manufacturer and she phoned him for samples of export quality carpet. The result was that we were able to purchase enough beautiful carpeting for the lounge, inner hall, front stairs and landing area. His bill came to £312!

I listened to Jean's prayers with greater respect after that!

There were also many gifts in materials and food. A hardware store owner sent us a van-load of all kinds of things from screws and nails to bathroom equipment. A well-wisher purchased a baby tractor with a rotary blade for cutting grass. Lionel and Moley Osborn always seemed to be finding tools or household furniture that they and their friends no longer required just when we needed them.

Local people were generous. Soon after the community arrived at Whatcombe the vicar of Winterborne Whitechurch, the Rev. Kingsley Laws, asked us to organise fortnightly prayer meetings for members of his congregation. These continued until our involvement with conferences made it impossible for us to act as hosts regularly to the group any more. Their gifts varied from boxes of eggs, vegetables and home-made cakes to a new deep-freeze.

With the donations were offers of practical help. People came in a steady flow during the summer and autumn of 1971 for a few days or a week. They were all ages and most denominations.

Jean's widowed mother, "Nan" Jillings, was one of our keenest helpers. Small in stature but astonishingly agile, she must have used her paintbrush in almost every room in the house! A teenage goddaughter spent a fortnight with us and at the end of the first week told me she had given her life to the Lord. A missionary, home on furlough, spent three days breaking up a concrete floor in a shower-room that was to be converted into a bathroom. A solicitor who was recovering from a nervous breakdown toiled with me for several days in dividing one room into two. An editor of a series of children's religious books decorated a long corridor during a week's holiday from her office.

How they slaved away, those casual helpers! Soon after an eight-thirty breakfast they were about the house with tools and paintpots. With only a short break for lunch and a breath of fresh air, they toiled through until five-thirty. Initially we met our helpers each evening for an hour's prayer and praise, but as the weeks went by we found ourselves getting so tired that it was difficult to keep awake after dinner.

In view of all the difficult tasks that were tackled, it was remarkable that no serious accident happened. The most serious was when I was scraping a cracked ceiling in a bedroom with two theological students in preparation for decorating. Without warning huge lumps of old plaster fell on us. We escaped with a few scratches and bruises.

There were plenty of shocks, frustrations and laughs.

The plumber, fixing pipes across the landing on the top floor of the main building, had to force open a cupboard that had been nailed up. When the door yielded, a small landslide of plaster and rubble, topped with the dried corpse of a blackbird, slid onto the floor, filling the air with dust.

It happened half-an-hour before the special dinner that had been prepared in honour of Mark's birthday. The rest of the community had bathed and put on suits and dresses. Only Ron and I were still in our working clothes, so we offered to deal with the mess while the others went on with the meal. We carried twelve dustbin-loads of rubbish down two floors and outside to the tip, while the clink of plates and bursts of laughter echoed up from the dining-room. Years before, a ceiling had collapsed in a bedroom on the top floor and lazy workmen, instead of getting rid of their rubbish, filled the cupboard with it and nailed up the door!

Because we were amateurs, we learned by our mistakes.

Reg hammered a nail into a bathroom wall and was hit in the face by a jet of cold water as he punctured a hidden pipe. The scene was worthy of a Chaplin comedy!

One wet day Ron left his shoes in the Aga to dry for a few minutes with the door open. Someone passing the kitchen just after he had gone saw the door open and slammed it shut without noticing the shoes. When Ron came back he found his shoes permanently curled up with the heat!

I spotted a handsome lampstand in a corner and, after being told that it did not belong to anyone, commandeered it for my room and repainted it. Later Lucia recognised it as one she had brought from Mersea and put in a corner for safety!

When winter arrived, the number of helpers dwindled, and for weeks the community worked alone. By now we were getting expert in doing most jobs quickly and efficiently, and the results were gratifying. For two or three weeks the house would look as if nothing was being accomplished — mess and dust everywhere — but then, suddenly, two more bedrooms, or a bathroom, or a staircase, would be completed and we would move on to the next stage of the work.

As each room was finished, we began to look forward to opening the house to guests. Talk round the meal-table shifted from discussions about colours for rooms and carpets for corridors to suggestons about the kind of conferences we would organise and the speakers we would invite.

Yet those months of preparation did more for us than get our home ready. They also prepared us to work as a team. The experience of labouring together as a strongly task-orientated group equipped us to face the difficulties we encountered when we began to run conferences. Although we were sometimes impatient because we had to do so much repairing and decorating, we saw later that this long period of practical work was one of the ways in which God drew us together before launching us into our corporate, spiritual ministry.

3

WE HAD INTENDED organising a number of small conferences while we continued the work on the house — thinking that we could earn an income to pay our way. But as the weeks went by and we realised that the repairs, alterations and decorations would require more of our time and energy than we had anticipated, we decided to press on with the practical tasks and not to open the house to conferences until the major jobs had been done. In December the members of the Fountain Trust Council used the house for one of their meetings, but they only needed five or six bedrooms. We fixed the official opening date for Easter 1972.

After Christmas we prepared the brochure and programme for 1972. Before arriving at Whatcombe we had adopted the name of "Barnabas Fellowship" for the community. We wanted to model our ministry on that of St. Barnabas. He is described in the book of Acts as a man "full of faith and of the Holy Spirit" and as "the encourager", the Spirit-filled follower of Jesus Christ who stood beside the other followers to support them and encourage them as they responded to the call of God. This is how we believed we were to be used in the Church — to stand beside and encourage other Christians as they sought God's will, and to lead them to a greater openness to the work of the Holy Spirit in their lives.

Eventually the packets of completed brochures arrived from the printers. Each brochure was a single folded sheet of paper. On the front were the words, "The Barnabas Fellowship, Whatcombe House, a Christian Centre" and an aerial photograph of the house and grounds. On the back we had a sketch-map of the road from Blandford to Winterborne Whitechurch and the lane that leads up to the entrances to our two drives. Inside was a short description of the community and another photograph. Accompanying the brochure, on a separate sheet of yellow paper, we had a list of our conferences for the period between Easter and Christmas. (We called it a "provisional list" because even then we were not sure that we would have everything ready!)

At the end of February eighteen members of the Lee Abbey community came to Whatcombe for a retreat (bringing with them a welcome gift of crockery from their stores). For us it was a dummy run — an opportunity to try out the house and our organisation for conference work. Since they were experts in this ministry — Lee Abbey welcomes thousands of guests in conferences all the year round — we felt that they would be sympathetic yet discerning critics.

They arrived in cars on the Wednesday in time for lunch. With mixed feelings — pride at the signs of what had been achieved mingled with anxiety that we might have forgotten something — we showed them their rooms.

Would they approve of the bright curtains and bedcovers, the flower arrangements and the hot-water-bottles, we wondered. Would they notice that the springs in some of the beds had lost their resilience, that the floors needed carpeting, and that the back staircase was in the shabby, broken state in which we had found it?

We had forewarned them that things might be rough and they came prepared with extra blankets, sleeping-bags and Arctic clothing — evidently expecting refugee-camp conditions! So maybe things were much better than they feared! Anyway, they wandered round the house expressing admiration and kindly ignored the defects they saw. The beginnings at Lee Abbey, we were told, had been much the same.

Silence was kept from the end of the evening sessions on Wednesday and Thursday until elevenses the following morning. During the meals we read them the moving story of Samuel Morris, the African boy who went to New York in the 1880s to learn about the Holy Spirit and who was used powerfully by God until his early death at the age of twenty-one.

Reg, Lucia and Jean spoke on Wednesday afternoon, telling our guests the way God had provided for us during our first months at Whatcombe. In the evening I gave a talk on prayer, and this led into a shortened form of Evensong followed by free praise and singing in the Spirit. On Thursday morning Ron spoke about spiritual renewal. During the afternoon we divided our guests into small groups and guided them in acts of meditation and silent prayer. In the evening there was a meeting for prayer and praise.

On Friday morning we celebrated the eucharist in the lounge. A table was placed in the centre of the new carpet, chairs arranged in a circle round it, and modern pictures hung up on the walls to illustrate the scripture readings. We used a stainless steel chalice and paten given to the community by Jeffrey Dodgson. We began the service by listening to a recording of chamber music played over David's stereo equipment. I read the introit psalm and collect, and David and Alma followed with the epistle and gospel. Between the readings one of the girls from Lee Abbey sang a solo accompanied by Rosemary on her guitar. Ray led the intercessions, and during the giving of the peace we joined hands and sang, "We are one in the Spirit". Everyone's hands were uplifted for the first part of the eucharistic prayer (from the Church of England's *Series Three Order for Holy Communion*) and the Sanctus and the acclamations were shouted with such fervour that they might have been heard at the bottom of the drive. After receiving Communion we kept silence again for several minutes, reading aloud one or two texts from the epistle and gospel as a guide to our corporate reflections.

We have celebrated many eucharists in the lounge at Whatcombe since that first one with the members of the Lee Abbey community, but already in that particular act of worship the distinctive character of our eucharists was beginning to emerge. We have always used as a basic outline the Church of England service but with a readiness to admit spontaneous variations and full participation so that each act of worship has been a fresh creation under the Holy Spirit.

The Lee Abbey retreatants left after lunch on Friday.

We waved goodbye as the cars rattled down the drive and sang, *Father, go with them*—a simple chorus Reg and Lucia had learned during their visit to the Mary Sisterhood at Darmstadt. Then we went back into the house, which felt curiously empty — back to the cleaning and decorating, back to the last preparations for the first official conference.

When we were tidying up the rooms next day, we found a piece of paper by one of the beds occupied by a girl from Lee Abbey. On it she had written:

Thank you.
God is my Father.
I am His child.
I am happy.

If everyone who comes to Whatcombe is led to the point where he or she can pray like that with sincerity, we thought, then we shall soon understand why the Lord has brought us here.

* * *

The following weekend, Friday, 25th February to Sunday, 27th February, was what we called "the invited conference". We wrote and invited to it those friends who had been closest to us in undertaking the foundation of the community. Cecil Cousen came to give the talks. We asked the Bishop of Salisbury, the Rt. Rev. J. E. Fison, to bless the house and the Fellowship.

At six o'clock on Friday evening all our guests were assembled—including the Bishop and Mrs. Fison, Desmond and Patricia Chichester, and the Rev. Kingsley

Laws and his wife, Kirsty—when an electricity cut blacked out the house! In the event, this proved to be an advantage. People chatted more freely in the informality forced on us by the emergency and, since we had not had time to decorate the dining-room, it looked better by candlelight!

After dinner, the Bishop put on his cassock and we gathered in the entrance hall for a short service of blessing.

"Except the Lord build the house, their labour is lost that built it."

We listened to the story of Mary and Martha read from the scriptures and the Bishop said a prayer of blessing for the house. Then we moved into the lounge singing a hymn. When everyone was seated, the Bishop prayed for the community. Dr. Fison had a gift for spontaneous prayer and our tape-recorder picked up his words:

> God the Father, God the Son, God the Holy Spirit, come amongst this community, every member of it, and endue them with the gifts of thy Spirit. Enable the members to live in love and charity with one another, and with all who visit this house.
>
> Give them the strength they need, the strength of body, mind and spirit. Send them forth from this house with their feet shod with the preparation of the gospel of peace.
>
> Give them perseverance and patience. Enable them daily to take up the cross of thine appointment, and may the living waters of the living God be spread abroad in the wastes and wilderness of our modern world.
>
> Give us hearts willing to respond to the glow of thy

fire. So set on fire this community living at Whatcombe that it may spread the message of thy love far and wide.

Draw into this fellowship those whom thou hast called to thy service. Save it from being centred upon itself. Inspire every member of it to venture to lose their lives that they may find them.

And raise up among us, O Lord we pray thee, through this Barnabas Fellowship, thy might, and come among us, and with great might and succour us, especially the Church in this locality and this diocese, through the inspiration of this community.

It was a solemn moment. When the prayer ended, I glanced round at the faces of the other members of the community; they looked slightly awed in the candlelight. Yet there was also a spirit of assurance among us — a confidence, not in ourselves, but in God. And when Reg spoke later on how we had come to Whatcombe and on how the Lord had provided for us and guided us since the previous summer, a feeling of deep thankfulness swept over us. We had learned in a new way what it meant to be under the hand of God.

A few months later Joe Fison died suddenly. While he was our Bishop, he took a personal interest in our community and told several people that its formation was one of the most encouraging things that had happened in his diocese during his episcopate. We were saddened by his unexpected death, but we were glad that during our first year we had had the support of one who, like our patron apostle, was a man filled with the Spirit of God.

4

In June 1972 Ken and Betty Taylor joined the community with their son, Jonathan, who was then eleven years old. (Their two eldest sons were married with homes and families of their own — David in South Africa, Peter at a theological college.) I have already described how they had been involved in a prayer group in Manchester with Ron and Jean and how they helped us during the summer of 1971. Ken brought his engineering and carpentry skills into the community; Betty took over responsibility for the office, acting as the warden's secretary and as the community's treasurer.

David and Alma left us in October the same year, having completed twelve months with us — the period they had set themselves when they came. David remained chairman of the trustees, so he and Alma continued to appear at Whatcombe every six months for the trustees' meetings.

Ray left us in May 1973 to return to sea. In June Rosemary married Jeffrey Dodgson, and they made their home near Basingstoke. The departure of these two youngest members of the Fellowship left the rest of us feeling middle-aged. Fortunately, this did not last for long!

Within a year of our establishment, we began to receive letters from people asking if they could join us. These requests forced us to work out more distinctly what was expected of a member of the Barnabas Fellowship, for only then could we explain our community to newcomers who had not been with us from the beginning.

By now it had become clear that there were two kinds of members in the Fellowship. There were those who believed that they had been called to Whatcombe for a lengthy period and those who believed that they had been called for one or two years. Reg and Lucia, Ron and Jean, and Ken and Betty belonged to the first category; the rest of us belonged to the second.

This variety in membership was, of course, very different from the traditional religious communities, most of whom require their members to take life vows after an extensive novitiate. The strength of this tradition is that everyone's commitment to the community is the same; like marriage, it is life-long. Its weakness is that it bars from membership those who could perhaps gain much personally from the experience of living in community for a few years and who could perhaps contribute uniquely to that community's life. This is why we did not make rules about the length of time a member should stay at Whatcombe.

Yet without long-term members, the Barnabas Fellowship would have lacked stability. If everyone had been thinking of leaving in six months, it would have been impossible to plan realistically for the years ahead. A community needs a strong minority of its members who are willing to commit themselves to its foreseeable future if it is to survive. They are like the parents of a family: they provide the rest of the group with a sense of permanence and security. Reg and Lucia, Ron and Jean, and Ken and Betty gave this to Whatcombe. By selling homes and resigning jobs, they demonstrated a single-minded obedience to God's call which acted as a foundation on which the Barnabas Fellowship was built.

The different kinds of membership — long-term and short-term — eventually threw up an important question. Should the short-term member of the community have as much authority in deciding the overall life and future of the Barnabas Fellowship as the long-term member? I do not think we ever framed the question precisely in those terms, but it was at the back of our minds when we discussed the future. It did not seem fair that the vote of the short-term member should affect decisions about matters in which he or she would not be involved in the years to come.

We resolved this problem by forming a Community Council. The Community Council consisted of the long-term members and the trustees. The Council met twice a year to decide projects for a major extension of the Fellowship's work involving financial commitments. Decisions were then put before the whole community where they could be ratified or referred back to the Council. On the whole, this system worked reasonably well. It gave the long-term members a feeling that they had more influence in the future planning of the community's life and activities and it relieved the short-term members of unfair responsibilities.

Otherwise, all members were treated alike. We drew

the same personal allowance in cash each month and we were each allowed four weeks' holiday away from Whatcombe each year. We had our own responsibilities about the house and in the work of the community. Teaching and counselling, catering, office work, household cleaning, gardening and maintenance — the departments soon emerged in our discussions and planning. Although individuals tended to specialise in one or two of these departments, we tried to be flexible and to help in any as the need arose.

It was fascinating to see a member of the community gradually develop new gifts. Some, who had come to Whatcombe thinking they would only be useful in practical work, were slowly involved in the teaching and counselling ministry during conferences. Others (including myself) who had been used to teaching and leading worship, found a new joy in tackling practical jobs about the house and garden. The experience of community enriched each one of us in this way.

During conferences our day was a long one. We met for prayers at six thirty. From seven thirty until eight thirty we were busy about the house, preparing breakfast, emptying bins, cleaning the hall, library and lounge, fetching the milk and the papers from the end of the drive, and getting ready for the day's activities.

Two or three of the community were generally engaged with the guests during the morning, speaking to the conference or leading group discussions. Others worked in the kitchen and in the house. After lunch had been served and most of the guests had gone out on walks or drives round the countryside, the house was quieter. We usually had some time to ourselves, but by tea time we were busy again.

Besides the business of preparing for and clearing up after tea and dinner, this was the time when there were group sessions and counselling interviews.

Most of the community tried to be present at the evening meetings, so it was half past ten or later before we could get to bed.

When there were no conferences — just over a third of the year — we met for prayers later — at eight thirty. The morning and the afternoon were occupied with tasks about the house and in preparation for the next conferences, but the evenings were free. This was the time when we could answer letters, watch the TV, and be more sociable with one another than we could be when we had a houseful of guests.

The process by which this simple structure of our life developed was not planned. We did not set out a blueprint for our life. Rather, the structure evolved during weeks of praying and discussing about our work, seeking the Lord's guidance through each problem as it presented itself.

* * *

This, then, was the kind of community to which people applied for membership.

When a letter arrived from such a person, Reg read it out to us. Some of the letters came from people who obviously did not realise what our work involved — invalids looking for a convalescent home, elderly folk thinking Whatcombe would be a nice place to retire to. The rest came from all kinds of Christians — young people leaving college, married couples with children, missionaries home from overseas, and clergy seeking an opportunity to experience community life.

We tried to discern those whom the Lord might be sending to us. These we invited to come and stay with us, preferably during a conference so that they could see Whatcombe when it was fully operational.

When they arrived, we each spent an hour or so with them. We invited them to join us in a practical task, (It was necessary to see what a person was like to work with as well as talk to, and we learned much about them as they gardened with us or helped with the washing-up!) Afterwards, we chatted with them over coffee in our rooms.

From this initial visit we decided whether or not to invite them to come for a longer period, perhaps a week or more, so that they could get to know us better and we could get to know them. If they did this, we were able to discuss with them more fully the possibility of their becoming a member of the Fellowship. Talking and praying together, we tried to help them to see if this was God's will for them and to puzzle out the problems connected with their homes, their families and their jobs.

Once this stage had been reached, the community was ready to decide whether or not a formal invitation should be made for them to join us for a six months' probationary period. This had to be a unanimous decision.

Liz Woolridge, a cousin of Rosemary, was the first to join us under this system. A New Zealander, she had worked in a variety of jobs in different parts of the world before she came to Whatcombe during Eastertime in 1973. She acted as an assistant in whatever department of the house required extra help — the office, the kitchen, or the domestic chores. Her literary skills were employed in the workshop-studios which we incorporated into our programmes during the longer conferences.

Trevor Walters joined us in September of that year. A school-teacher who had spent a year at the Mayflower Family Centre in Canning Town, he had been to Whatcombe as a casual helper on a number of occasions. He assisted Ron and Ken in the practical work about the house. Between them, they were responsible for nearly all the improvements at Whatcombe during the next two years, including the decorating of the community dining-

room, the equipping of the laundry, the conversion of a store into a play-room for children, and the alterations needed to change an old generator building into a two-roomed bungalow.

After Ray had returned to sea, Lucia took charge of the kitchen, cooking for the community and its guests. With her other work, this threw a considerable strain on her, and we prayed earnestly for another cook. Our prayers were answered in November that year when Margaret Bradley came from the community at Scargill to take over this task. She brought with her fresh ideas about community living — and new items on the menu!

After Margaret Bradley's arrival, the membership remained static for nearly a year. Then, in October 1974, I married Margaret Wood. I had intended leaving Whatcombe before my marriage, but as the Lord seemed to make no opening for me, Reg kindly suggested that I should stay on at Whatcombe for a time and that Margaret should join us. This we did. Margaret left her work at the Queen Elizabeth School of Nursing in Birmingham and bravely accepted the double rôle of being my wife and a member of the Fellowship! We lived in the bungalow I have just mentioned — one of the most beautiful little homes a newly-wed couple could have — and so enjoyed a certain amount of privacy in the midst of community life.

The following year, 1975, there were a number of changes. Trevor left to train at Salisbury and Wells Theological College. Liz returned to New Zealand. In the summer Maureen Allchin joined us, bringing with her several years' experience in teaching at a comprehensive school in Ealing. Then David and Valerie Thorpe, a young couple, came to Whatcombe from London where David had worked as a glazier for the Newham Borough Council and Valerie had been employed by Dr Barnardo's.

This is how the membership of the community changed during the four years described in this book. When a member left, the rest of us missed him a good deal. Life felt different. Jobs had to be shuffled round and routines changed. But the arrival of a new person brought a fresh inspiration and novel insights to our corporate ministry. We were fortunate in that our change-over in membership was gradual.

Discussing possible applicants, we often asked ourselves how far we should be influenced in our choice by our ideas about the kind of skills we needed in the community.

For example, with the house we rented about nine acres of ground. We were able to do little with it except mow the lawn and tend the flowerbeds, and in our prayers we asked the Lord to send us a gardener who could cultivate our walled garden and supply us with fresh vegetables, fruit and salads. Yet during these years, no such person was sent.

I do not know the answer to this problem. All I can suggest is that, if the individual concerned and the community have a firm conviction that God is calling that person to join them, then his or her gifts and skills will find full employment. Maybe the Lord had his own reasons for not allowing us to spend too much time and money on our grounds during our early years!

After six months' probation, the candidate was admitted as a full member of the Barnabas Fellowship and given the community's emblem to wear. We devised a short service for the occasions. It reflects, I think, our picture of ourselves as a community within the Church of Jesus Christ.

ADMISSION TO FULL MEMBERSHIP OF THE BARNABAS FELLOWSHIP

During a Service of Holy Communion.

Bible Readings: Colossians 3: 12–17
John 17: 6–19

THE WARDEN: *N., you have lived with us for ... and, during this time, you have sought the Lord's will for your future. We, too, have prayed that you will be guided by Him. Do you believe that it is His will that you should join us as a full member of the Barnabas Fellowship?*

THE CANDIDATE: *I do.*

THE FELLOWSHIP: *N., you have committed yourself to God through union with Christ by prayer and personal growth in holiness. Will you also commit yourself to us as to a family in the Family of God, for the work to which our heavenly Father has called us; that is, to be those who, like St. Barnabas, are encouragers in the Body of Christ, so that the children of God's Family are full of faith and of the Holy Spirit?*

THE CANDIDATE: *I will, the Lord being my helper.*

THE WARDEN then holds the Candidate by the hand and says: *N., we admit you as a full member of the Barnabas Fellowship with glad hearts, in the Name of the Father and of the Son and of the Holy Spirit. Amen.*

He hands the new member the Fellowship emblem, saying: *Receive this as long as you remain among us, as a sign that you will live in the power of Jesus Christ, crucified and risen, and in the fellowship of the Holy Spirit.*

THE WARDEN and THE FELLOWSHIP together: *We renew our commitment to God through union with Christ by prayer and personal growth in holiness; we renew our commitment to each other, and to you, N., our new member, as servants of God in the Barnabas Fellowship, in the Name of the Father, and of the Son, and of the Holy Spirit.*

The new member then gives the 'peace' to the Warden and the members of the Fellowship, and any others present.

5

"It's so peaceful here," said a guest to me one day.

She was standing on the steps outside the main doors of Whatcombe, gazing at the beautiful sweep of parkland and trees that surround the slopes below the house.

"It must be like living in paradise," she continued. "I'm sure you don't know what it is to have tensions among yourselves."

Her inaccuracy was so gross that I could not restrain myself.

"Indeed we do!" I blurted out with feeling.

Her eyes widened, her expression changed. If I had uttered a blasphemy, she could not have looked more shocked. Then she walked away. Her vision of paradise had gone!

Except for the six months that Lucia had been a member of the community at Lee Abbey before her marriage, none of us who arrived at Whatcombe in the summer of 1971 had had much experience of communal living. We had heard that some had found this sort of thing a strain, but we did not think that this was likely to happen to us. After all, we told ourselves, hadn't the Lord brought us together? And weren't we all good friends?

Looking back, I remember that the first tiny manifestation of a tension came to me on the day I joined the Fellowship. I was driving down to Whatcombe when I mentioned to Lucia (whom I had picked up in London) that I would have to go back to the city the following week to attend a meeting.

'You'll have to see if the community'll let you," she said.

She had half-intended it as a joke, but there was enough truth in her remark for me to realise, with a small sense of shock, that I was no longer free to do what I wanted to do. My activities were to be circumscribed by the opinions and needs of eight other people.

Gradually each one of us began to realise this restriction. It was not that anyone in the Fellowship wanted me or any other member to be confined by them. On the contrary, we would urge each other to be free to do what was considered right. But any group of people, if they are to live and work together, inevitably impose restrictions on the inclinations of individuals — usually subconsciously — and this sense of being confined by the rest is sensed by all.

It was a curious phenomenon. It was so different from what we had experienced before. In our former homes with parents, wives, husbands and children, familiarity and flexibility had tended to mollify the restrictions placed on us by being a member of a family. In our places of work we had learned to accept the limitations imposed on us as part of the job. (We left them behind when we went home, anyway!) But in a new community, and in a larger grouping than any of us had ever lived in before, the tensions caused by not knowing whether or not certain signs of independence would be acceptable to the rest were considerable. There were times when, because of these tensions, Whatcombe seemed more like a prison than a home.

A typical illustration is provided by an incident that Jean recalled one day when we were discussing this problem. During the early weeks at Whatcombe, Jean had gone into Blandford on one occasion to do some shopping. Coming back through a country lane that follows the ridge of an escarpment, she had stopped the car for a few minutes and got out to admire the view. While she was standing there, another car came along the road from Blandford and whisked past her. Suddenly she realised that it was the same kind of car as that driven by Reg. A little cold hand seemed to clutch her heart. Had it been Reg? What would he think of her, apparently wasting time?

When she got back to Whatcombe, she discovered that Reg had not left the house all day. Her fear had been groundless. Yet it was the kind of fear of one another that we often experienced, and no matter how we tried to analyse each fresh situation, we were never able to trace its origin. It lay somewhere in that area of our relationships where we did not trust one another sufficiently. As long as any member of the Fellowship had a question in his or her mind about the way another member used the community's time and resources, then somewhere, somehow, that question would create a tension with its accompanying fear. It was a long time before the Holy Spirit dealt with these fears as we grew closer to one another in the love of Jesus Christ.

Another tension was caused by differences in our rôle-expectations of one another.

Reg, as warden, had a picture of himself in that rôle which did not match the pictures that others had of him. Having initiated the community, he assumed a certain authority only to discover that his decisions were sometimes challenged by some, if not all, of the Fellowship. The result of this was that he tended for several months to retreat to a position where he felt he could not suggest anything — a position which was all the more difficult for him when he realised that things were likely to go wrong because decisions about them had not been made. He found himself paralysed, unable to act in ways he felt a warden should be able to act for the good of the community.

During the practical work in preparing the house, Ron, appointed sub-warden, was our unquestioned overseer. We were happy to labour under his patient direction because he had considerable ability in both tackling the jobs that needed to be done and in encouraging others to tackle them. But when the first stage of the practical work was over, his status changed. He found that he did not have the same authority as he had had during the early months. He felt that the rest of the community was still tending to treat him as the one responsible for the practical work about the house, whereas he saw himself involved in the ministry of teaching and counselling during conferences.

The problem of rôle-expectations was experienced by all of us in different ways. After being a vicar for thirteen years and virtually free to shape my activities as I felt led, I now found myself expected to share in the mundane tasks needed to look after our guests. Ray, formerly a ship's cook and master of his own kitchen, had to learn how to prepare meals in a kitchen invaded by women and children under the general supervision of Lucia.

For the women special difficulties arose. Lucia, Jean, Alma and Betty had all been wives and mothers in their own homes for many years. To have to share something of those rôles with other women was quite a strain for each of them. Individually they might have been relieved at the freedom of not having to prepare meals every day, but to be unable to cook a favourite dish for her husband and family for months on end was a severe deprivation!

Varying standards and tastes in the hundred-and-one little things that made up the business of daily living enlarged the strain. In the average natural family these standards and tastes are passed on from mothers to daughters and are usually accepted (even if daughters change once they have their own homes); but put three or four wives together and the differences are felt immediately. There was always an inclination for one to say, "I would never cook it that way," or, "I would never choose that colour for a bathroom". The mothers in the Fellowship felt that they were being robbed of the responsibilites of motherhood when others prepared their children's meals or did things for their families that they would normally do themselves.

* * *

Then there were the tensions caused by our differing personalities and Christian traditions. Some were used to expressing their thoughts and feelings forthrightly; others were more reserved. Some came from an evangelical background, others from the broad and high church traditions of the Church of England.

We had known, of course, that these differences might create problems and we were prepared for them (though they are greater when people live, pray and work together every day than if they are encountered in a church meeting). What we were not prepared for were the deeper, psychological problems hiding like rocks under the surface of the sea. Roughly speaking, these deeper problems came from two factors: (1) that we were living in a closer intimacy with others than we had experienced before, outside our immediate families, and (2) that our Fellowship contained both married and single people.

Put like that, it might sound as if we were unbelievably naïve. Perhaps we were. But there are some things that you cannot learn from books, or even from the experience of others. You have to discover them for yourself. And it was only in experiencing the tensions of being together that we began to learn about the deeper problems of community living.

Let us take the factor of being in a closer intimacy with others first. When an individual joins a community, he begins to re-live the experience of belonging to a family as the relationships in the community become more intimate. If that individual has not had the opportunity of establishing a mature relationship with his parents and family before he left home, he will have to cope with the problem of unresolved conflicts as they arise in his relationships with other members of the community.

The most familiar example of this is found in the relationship between a newly-wedded couple. During times of tension between them, the husband, or the wife, or both, will tend to react towards one another like aggressive children or discontented teenagers. If the source of these reactions are not recognised, they can be very destructive; but as the couple mature in their relationship, the unresolved conflicts are worked through and their marriage grows in strength and trust.

In a community, where we are relating not just to one other person but to several, this tendency towards conflict is considerably aggravated. At Whatcombe nine or ten of us were having not only to live with one another but also work each day alongside each other. Inevitably there were occasions when the ordinary circumstances of our life and work caused us to disagree among ourselves. In the tensions generated by these disagreements, each of us found ourselves reverting to the aggressiveness of youth.

I noticed this especially during the first year in my attitudes towards Reg and Ron. For example, during an animated discussion with Reg one day, I felt my temper rising and I suddenly heard myself calling him "Dad"! Later, on reflection, I realised what had happened. Some unresolved conflict in my teenage past had come up from my subconscious and I had slipped back into one of those occasions when, as a rebellious teenager, I had argued with my parent over what I should or should not be allowed to do.

Through the rise and fall of tensions, we slowly learned what unexpected impulses and fears can be released within us as we are drawn into new experiences of intimate, corporate life. Our personalities were more exposed to one another than we had known before — except, perhaps, with a parent or a spouse. Fearing greater exposure of ourselves, we reacted in the way I have described. But once that fear of exposure was gone, then our relationships with one another deepened. We came to see that one of the most important pastoral tasks within a community is that members should help one another to work through these tensions and fears, for it is only in this way that the life of the community is strengthened.

The second factor — that we consisted of both married and single members — did not strike us as particularly significant at first. This was probably because we thought and spoke of our community as one family. But gradually the differences began to make themselves felt. The married couples found that they had to adjust in their relationships with one another in a community setting. With seven or eight other people around them every day, husbands and wives experienced considerable strains between themselves. They had been hospitable in their own homes before coming to Whatcombe, and they were used to having people about. But a guest in a private home is not the same as sharing a large house with others who have as much right to be there as you have!

Those who were parents also felt themselves increasingly torn between being involved in community activities at conference time and giving more attention to their children. This affected Reg and Lucia, and Ken and Betty, in the first years, when their children were younger. Mark, Catherine and Jonathan naturally did not want to share in many of the conference sessions — which usually involved their parents in the evenings and at weekends when they were home from school.

Then there was the constant test of loyalties — to a husband or a wife or a child who was feeling the strain of community living on the one side, and to the community of which you were a member on the other. And often you knew that your husband (wife, child) was in the wrong!

The difficulty encountered by the unmarried was in the feeling that they sometimes experienced of being "second-class" members of the Fellowship. I want to stress here, before I say any more, that this was not shared by all the single people all the time. I also want to stress that, as far as the rest of the community was concerned, this feeling was a complete fantasy. There was never any intention that the single members should be treated any differently from the married members.

Yet, fantasy though it may have been, the unmarried member did experience this feeling, particularly when his or her personal interests conflicted with the interests of the community.

It was partly due to the fact that the single members had had, on the whole, more independence than the married members before they came to Whatcombe. In the community they had to learn to submit to other people's needs — meals had to be fixed to fit in with the timing of the school bus, days off arranged to meet the requirements of families. Also, at Whatcombe the single members tended to feel more cut off from their friends. On days off the married members had each other's company, whereas the single members did not always want to go out with each other.

But these circumstances only partially accounted for the

sense of being "second-class" members. Underneath them was the basic psychological difference between the married and the unmarried — that is, when brought into intimate relationships with married couples, single people almost always feel at a personal disadvantage, no matter how loving and accepting those relationships may be.

During those four years I had the experience of being both single and married in the community; and, although I did not find it easier in one state than the other, I did find I gained considerable strength in my relationship with the rest of the community when I was able to share it with my wife. It was rather like the difference between standing on one leg and standing on two.

Although my wife's relationship with the community developed in her own way (and in a community it is vital that married couples should allow each other to establish their own relationship with the rest), yet we had a security in our togetherness that helped to make us more secure in the Fellowship. Without this, a single member tends to feel less secure (and therefore "second-class"), at least until his or her relationship with the community has matured over years of corporate life.

Perhaps some readers will be a little shocked by these revelations — like the visitor I mentioned at the beginning. Folk expect a "charismatic" community to be a peaceful, joyful crowd! Yet I see now that had we not experienced these difficulties, we could not have ministered to others when they came to us with their own problems. We would have become so complacent that we would have been useless to everyone else. Instead, we had to recognise our real weaknesses and to depend totally upon God, to learn what it means to be reconciled to God through Jesus Christ and to be built into unity by the Holy Spirit.

The result was that when people came to Whatcombe they *did* find peace and joy and unity. But this atmosphere was not our doing. It was the grace of the Holy Spirit himself, working in the community and overflowing into the lives of those who stayed with us.

How God began to do this I will outline in the next chapter.

6

"I HOPE THEY STAY TOGETHER," said Joe Fison to a friend, shortly after he had attended the invited conference at Whatcombe in 1972. The Bishop knew something of the difficulties which small communities experience in the early months of their existence. As far as the Barnabas Fellowship was concerned, his hopes were justified. We did stay together. But there were two or three occasions when the tensions caused by the problems described in the last chapter might well have split the community if the Lord had not poured his unifying love abundantly on us during difficult times in the first two years.

Undergirding all that we did at Whatcombe was the conviction that God had brought us together from different parts of England for his purpose. The astonishing provision of help, materials and money that enabled us to commence our ministry was, to us, a tangible sign of his blessing.

It is an ancient spiritual truth that the Christian recognises the grace of God in the present by recounting his blessings in the past. Many of our first guests asked us to tell them how the Fellowship had come together and how

God had provided for us in the first months at Whatcombe — the story I have told in chapters one and two of this book. As we listened to one another retelling the familiar story, we found ourselves encouraged by the knowledge that God had a purpose for us. Little did those guests know what their requests to hear that story meant to us as a community!

Sometimes, after a day of depression or downheartedness, I would sit in the lounge with the rest of the Fellowship and our guests feeling that there was nothing of the spirit of praise left in me. The choruses were mockery to my ears; the prayers empty and meaningless. Then Reg or Ron, Lucia or Jean, would step forward and begin to tell the tale — how Reg and Lucia had been led to believe they would be called into community life, how they had met Ron and Jean at High Leigh, how they had been offered Whatcombe, and so on. I knew it so well that I could almost repeat the words with them. Yet every time, as I listened, I experienced a lightening of my heart and a quickening of my faith, and by the time they had finished, I was ready to join in the next chorus with thankfulness. I know now why the children of Israel were instructed to repeat the story of the exodus each year at the Passover. It was not merely to pass on the folklore of their race to their children. It was to be a living memorial of what the Lord had done and could do with a strong hand!

So it was not pride that held us together, nor was it fear of failure. It was the encouragement that God gave us through one another, even in the midst of the acutest tensions.

This encouragement came especially during our

prayers. During those hours when we met together to reflect upon the Word of God and to offer our confessions, our petitions and our praise, we experienced the unifying love of the Lord most powerfully. However critical I may have been about our prayer time — as I will indicate presently — the overriding blessing was that it maintained an openness to God in the community which enabled him to begin to triumph over the divisive forces which we felt in living and working together.

Morning after morning we faced each other in a circle, Bibles in hand. You cannot nurse a grievance against somebody when you have to read the scriptures and pray with him every day like this. Furthermore, you cannot hide your feelings. The rest of the community know you so well that they can discern in a few moments when you are wallowing in self-pity or bending under a problem. And, in a curious way, you know they know! You cannot hide it! You are stripped of pretence!

For all of us this was initially a humiliating experience. But it was the beginning of healing in the community. It demonstrated the scriptural truth of where we find repentance and forgiveness. The individual Christain knows the accepting forgiveness of God when he acknowledges his true condition before him — his sinfulness. Similarly, as individual members of the community, we learned that healing began when we acknowleged before one another what we really were. And it was in being accepted by the rest of the community for what we really were that the love of God flowed through them to us. This is how self is dethroned and Christ enthroned in the midst of our Christian brothers and sisters.

The practical application of this loving and trusting had to be worked out in the day-to-day activities of the Fellowship, from the mundane duties around the house, office and garden, to the intensive ministry of talking, listening and leading in worship during busy conferences.

In my relationships with the rest of the community, I slowly learned to try and stand aside from myself when I felt any tension and to go through a process of self-examination. It worked out something like like this:

(1) Check the apparent cause of the tension with the reality of the situation. I realised how easy it was for a fantasy to build up in my mind, attributing to others attitudes or motives that were far from what they really felt or thought.

(2) Ask the Lord to illuminate my heart to see if the tension is caused by something within myself. The devil is a master in the art of taking a personal failing and twisting it into a feeling of self-righteous indignation against the rest of the community or a member of it!

(3) Interpret every remark and every action by another in the best possible way. In the spirit of Christ's love, assume that they did not intend to be hurtful in what they said, or disruptive in what they did, unless the evidence to the contrary is irrefutable.

(4) If, after taking these steps, the apparent cause of the tension is still associated with one of the community, go and discuss the matter with the individual concerned at an appropriate moment — not when he or she is busy or tired.

(5) If the apparent cause of the tension lies within the whole community, bring the matter up with them all, but

do it remembering that Jesus Christ is in the midst of them.

Readers will recognise these steps as a practical application of Matthew 18: 15–20.

How important it is to have time to talk things through! In the busy early months and when the conferences began, there were always so many practical things to be done that it seemed at first to be a waste of precious hours sitting and discussing our problems. It was easier to be doing than to be listening! And, to be frank, some of us were tempted to escape into activity in order to forget the problems that we sensed in us and around us.

But we gradually came to realise that we must set aside periods when we could talk together as a group, and it was out of this realisation that the weekly community meeting was inaugurated. We gave it a high priority in our programme and guarded it against the intrusion of other demands made on us as individuals and as a group.

The community meeting usually lasted two hours or so; occasionally we extended it to a whole day. In it we discussed and planned every aspect of community life, from our days off during the following week to the details of next year's conference programme. From the point of view of business efficiency, we probably wasted a lot of time. Our discussions would have been tidier and our decisions would have been more effective if we had had prepared agendas and duplicated minutes. But, in our situation, the untidiness of our community meetings gave them an informality that was necessary. They would not have been so homely if they had been more businesslike.

Reg referred everything to the community meeting,

even questions about whether or not a guest should be permitted to stay on for an extra night after a conference had finished. This meant that our decision-making process was a rather cumbersome affair, but it had the effect of involving every member of the Fellowship in all aspects of its life, so that if, for example, a certain guest did stay on for an extra night after a conference, we all felt a measure of responsibility for him.

We sometimes got impatient with one another, but most meetings were enjoyable occasions of fellowship. In busy conferences they were the only time when every member of the community was present (days off usually meant that at least one or two were absent from the community prayers during the week.) Often they were times when I knew that I would receive the wisdom and encouragement of God through my friends when I discussed with them various plans and attendant problems. To be able to seek God's will for myself in reaching some of the more important decisions of my life with a group of Christian friends whom I could trust completely is a privilege that too few experience in local churches today.

* * *

As we grew together, so we learned to accept responsibility for pastoral leadership in the community. First, we had to allow Reg to exercise authority as warden. Then he was able to develop into the kind of leader who encourages and enables others to fulfil their ministry within the on-going life of the Fellowship. Sometimes this was rather a tight-rope act for him. On the one hand there was perhaps an individual member who was eager to initiate a new project; on the other hand there were the other members of the community, settled into a smoothly-running routine and resisting changes that might upset a system they had got used to over months and years (a not unfamiliar problem for any Christian leader!).

Secondly, we had to allow Ron to develop his rôle as sub-warden as he felt the Lord lead him. This involved him in training for ordination under the auxiliary pastoral ministry scheme at Salisbury and Wells Theological College. Eventually he emerged as a fellow-elder with a teaching and pastoral ministry rather than just as one who was responsible for the maintenance of the building.

And, thirdly, we had to accept responsibilities for pastoral leadership ourselves. It might be necessary for any one of us to make decisions on behalf of the rest of the community, from the purchase of goods during a shopping expedition to a radical change in a conference programme if an emergency cropped up, and we could only do this as we gave each other encouragement and confidence to act on behalf of the whole Fellowship.

I have already described the kinds of tension that were sometimes felt among the married and single members of the community. In tackling this problem we came to realise that, much as we would like to think of ourselves as one large family, we were in fact a number of separate families and that to try and gloss over the natural relationship between husbands, wives and children was to damage the heart of our community life. To pretend that the married relationship was subordinate to the community relationships was intolerable. As Jean said with spirit one day, she was not going to be like the woman of Samaria, with five husbands instead of one!

From 1974 we arranged for the single members to be "adopted" into the families of the married members. At that time Margaret Bradley became part of the East family, Trevor Walters part of the Dodgson family, and Liz Wool-ridge part of the Taylor family. (Since I was about to be married, I was not "adopted"!) In practice this meant that Margaret, Trevor and Liz could share the sitting-rooms of their respective "families" when they wanted to, spend some days off with them, and occasionally go on holiday with them. This did much to ease the sense of being "second-class" members of the Fellowship, and what might have been an over-emphasis on our oneness was balanced by a healthy recognition that natural family groupings had to be respected in community life.

These, then, were some of the ways in which we tried to solve the problems caused by living in community. I am not claiming that we solved them completely. Wherever people live, pray and work together there will always be tensions of one kind or another. But I believe that through the process of seeking solutions to problems we matured under God to be able to exercise a ministry to others by the power of the Spirit. Inasmuch as we were victorious, Jesus Christ was glorified.

7

THE LIFE OF ANY Christian community receives its inspiration and upbuilding from its corporate prayer. This is the lesson which has been learned by the Church from New Testament times. When the apostolic Church in Jerusalem was faced with opposition to its preaching, they prayed together and were filled with the Holy Spirit to speak the word of God with greater boldness.

As a parish priest in the Church of England, I had been accustomed to saying the offices of Morning and Evening Prayer either in church or at home. When I was a member of a staff, I said the offices with the other clergy; when I was a vicar I said Morning and Evening Prayer alone or with any of the congregation who cared to join me. The orderly recitation of the psalter, the systematic reading of the Old and New Testaments, and the use of canticles and collects had been the foundation of my spirituality since the days when I was a student. Round it there grew up my own meditations and prayers — and when meditating and praying were difficult, there was always the office to be said to direct my thoughts towards God.

I had gone down to Whatcombe assuming that the community's prayers would take a similar form. It was, therefore, a disappointment to me to discover that the members who had already established themselves in the house were spending an informal hour together, reading the Bible and praying spontaneously in what seemed to me to be a very unliturgical and un-office-like manner. I was critical of this pattern for several months and it was more than a year before I got used to it.

This is an illustration of the ways in which different traditions in the community jarred against one another. I had been brought up in the high church tradition of the Church of England, and from my college days I had been taught that the proper form of corporate prayer for Christians was the daily office. But at Whatcombe I had to learn that Matins and Evensong are only one of many possible forms of daily devotion for Christians, and that our reading of the Bible and spontaneous prayer were just as much part of the Christian heritage as the services of the Prayer Book.

The breakthrough came for me, strangely enough, outside Whatcombe. While I was a member of the community, I went to Salisbury one day a week to teach liturgy at the theological college. It was there that I encountered widespread dissatisfaction with the daily office among the students and a longing for more informal corporate prayer. And it was there, as we studied the history of the liturgy together, that I discovered (what I had forgotten since my own theological college days) that the Church's earliest prayers were probably spontaneous and that it is a mistake to contrast too sharply liturgical prayer with unstructured prayer. Furthermore, the movement for liturgical reform in the Church of England, in the Roman Catholic Church and in some of the Reformed Churches, is attempting to blend free prayer with liturgical forms in new services.

All this helped me to accept the community's form of daily prayer. During those four years at Whatcombe, I came to see how the Holy Spirit can inspire a petition or an act of praise that is just as worthy of Almighty God as anything out of a treasury of devotions. And I also came to appreciate in a new way the familiar prayers of the liturgy, especially when we could use them within an on-going flow of praise and intercession that did not depend too much on reading formularies from a book.

However, any routine of corporate prayer, liturgical or spontaneous, can create personal problems from time to time for those who participate in it. We go through periods when everything seems dull and uninspiring. Often this has nothing to do with the routine itself but with something in ourselves. During prayers with the community, the rebellious feelings tend to rise to the surface. There were several occasions when I did not utter a word at community prayers for a week or longer because I was feeling in revolt against the other members or because I had a conflict within myself that had not been fully resolved.

When we use a formal structure, the effect of individual feeling is to some extent neutralised because everyone is given a certain amount of set liturgical material to sing or to say and, even in one's worst moments, it requires little effort to join in. But when nearly all the prayer is spontaneous, relying on each member's initiative and inspiration, then the effect of one individual's personal feelings is soon sensed by the rest of the community. I always knew when one of the Fellowship was struggling with a problem, for a sense of heaviness fell on the group during prayers. Heaviness of this kind was difficult to shake off — though it lifted when someone else opened himself or herself to the Holy Spirit in an act of praise, in English or in tongues, into which the rest of us could be caught up.

The advantage of unstructured prayer on these occasions was that, when a spirit of heaviness was felt, we could sometimes abandon our routine and talk and pray the matter through with those concerned. I can remember a number of mornings when we did not "pray" (in the sense of addressing God directly) much at all. Instead, we shared among ourselves the things that were burdening us and only at the end committed our conversation briefly to the Lord. It was then that I saw how healing and comforting our type of community prayers could be.

The daily Bible reading and our corporate reflection upon the scriptures served to draw out from us our different Christian traditions. There were mornings when the tensions brought about by widely variant interpretations of the scriptures were almost too much to bear. But out of it emerged a deep unity with each other in the Holy Spirit — a unity which enabled us to see beyond theological differencces to a true oneness with each other in the love of Jesus Christ. This was true ecumenism. And, as an additional bonus, the scriptures came alive for me in a fresh way as I learned, from the evangelical members of the community, how to listen to the Lord speaking to us through the Spirit from the ancient texts.

* * *

Let me describe an average community prayer meeting. My room, before my marriage, was on the same landing as the Easts', and soon after six o'clock I heard Reg go into the tiny kitchen near his bedroom, fill and switch on the electric kettle, and put the mugs on a tray. It was a sign for me that it was time to get up. By six thirty we were gathering in the Easts' sitting-room, Reg handing round the mugs of tea. (He made this his service to the community each day before prayers and there can have been few other things that he has done for us that have been appreciated more!)

Each week one of the community led the prayers. The shape of the morning varied according to the leader's wishes. There might be a period of silence at the beginning, or a short discussion, or a psalm or a hymn. Then the one who was reading — a different member of the Fellowship each day — announced the scriptural passage, read it, and made a few comments on it.

The conversation which followed might drift a long way from the topic introduced by the reading. Personal opinions were aired, differences of viewpoint revealed, experiences shared. Usually at the end of the half hour, the leader brought the discussion to a close, and we settled down to a further thirty minutes of free prayer.

A few sentences of praise — silence — a verse of a chorus or psalm — more silence — a few petitions following one another round the group — a wisp of humour and a murmur of laughter — and more silence — a request for the laying-on of hands for healing because one of the Fellowship had a bad cold, bringing one or two of us to our feet to move over and minister to the individual who had made the request — a longer silence — concentrated intercession for a few minutes for a particular need we had met with in one of our guests at the conference — the leader closing with the Lord's Prayer and a morning collect.

Occasionally there were surprises — beautifully formulated acts of praise coming spontaneously from one member, snatches of song, brief but inspiringly apt quotations from the scriptures, a picture described to the Fellowship — so that we could never be sure where the Spirit was going to lead us each morning. And although there were some days when I felt that the half hour would never end, there were others when the time fled by as if it had been only a few minutes — a brief entry into eternity.

Our community prayers were sometimes held in the chapel.

The possibility of having a chapel came when we inspected more carefully the cellars of the house. When we arrived these were the horrors of the place. We could hardly bear to think of them for months. The stairs down to them were worn and dangerous, the oil-fired boilers roared in one cellar, and the rest of the cellars were dark, damp and filthy.

One cellar was particularly daunting. Square-shaped in plan, it had a central column supporting the ceiling, and it was filled shoulder-high with dust and rubbish, stuff that had been dumped in it over many years. But as we looked at it through the gloom, it revealed itself as a possible chapel. It could be a beautiful place if it were cleaned up, we thought.

The process of cleaning and decorating the cellar and the steps down to it began in 1972. When the chamber was cleared, it turned out to be one of the most striking rooms in the house. The graceful curves of the arches supporting the ceiling merged into the central column and beneath the dirty whitewash on the walls were the warm red eighteenth-century bricks and flintwork. The neat proportions gave the cellar an atmosphere of harmony and peace.

A young couple from Mersea spent a weekend heroically in the choking task of scraping the whitewash from the walls. David and Alma completed the job. The dust it made was appalling. No one could work in it for more than twenty minutes. David tried various experiments with vacuum cleaners to make the air more bearable. In the end he and Alma toiled with damp cloths round their mouths.

Round the cellar was a low shelf, built of bricks and evidently used for storage purposes. We were given some pews from a disused Methodist church; Ken renovated these and fixed them to the shelving to provide seating for about twenty-five people. Ron filled the two windows in with glass bricks. Rush matting was laid on the floor and a table-top fastened to the central column made an altar.

The late Canon Harold Wilson, then principal of the Salisbury and Wells Theological College, gave us a beautiful wood-carving of Christ with arms outstretched as if on the cross surrounded with a madela of cloud. The crucifixion — the resurrection — the ascension — the second coming — all were portrayed by this remarkable work of art. It filled one of the arches on the side wall of the chapel perfectly.

Reg celebrated the first eucharist on All Saints' Day, 1972, and from that time we started using the chapel for

eucharists on Wednesdays and Fridays out of conference time.

From that time, also, a little more formality came into our community prayers. We used parts of *Series Three* for the eucharists and parts of Morning Prayer on some other days. The balance was, I believe, welcomed by all. Early problems disappeared, and there were many mornings when we could say, with Peter on the mount of transfiguration, "Lord, it is good for us to be here."

8

DURING THE MONTHS OF 1971–72, while we were working on the house, we often looked forward to and talked about what Ron called "the job that the Lord has sent us here for". Reg's vision of a small community, whose life together was rooted in prayer and who would encourage other members of the Church through conferences and similar gatherings, would then have to be worked out in practical terms. Would members of the Church respond to the ministry that was being offered to them at Whatcombe? we asked ourselves. Fortunately, Reg and Lucia had a wide circle of friends and acquaintances who by now knew about the new community and who had shown an interest in it. Soon after we had sent the first brochures out, the applications began to flow back. They have continued to flow back ever since. During these four years we only had to cancel three conferences because the numbers applying to come did not justify the expense of proceeding with the arrangements.

About two hundred and ten days of each year were occupied with conferences. We were never entirely happy with the title as a description of the gatherings on which our ministry as a community was based. It sounded much too formal. "House-party" was not a felicitous alternative, for it could suggest only fun and games! One year we called two of our conferences "celebrations" but we were told afterwards that these titles had put some off because they were not sure what the titles meant!

The subjects for the conferences were mostly on the charismatic renewal and matters arising from it. A number of weekends each year were entitled "Baptism in the Spirit": to these came Church folk interested in personal renewal. There were conferences on the implication of personal renewal for the individual as a member of a congregation: "Ministry in the Spirit", "Renewal in the Local Church", "Pentecost in the Parish". And there were conferences on the gift of healing in its widest connotation: "The Ministry of Healing", "Christian Maturity", "Emotional Problems and Christian Wholeness". During these four years I saw a shift in our emphasis towards topics related to the charismatic renewal as it affected Church life.

These topics were to some extend dictated by popular demand. We did not relish the idea of being thought of as a "charismatic" community (surely any Christian group must be truly charismatic?) and we insisted that we were at Whatcombe to teach the whole counsel of God. With this in view we included in our first programmes conferences on "non-charismatic" subjects such as liturgy and mission.

But the response to these was disappointing. From the demand indicated by the number of returned application forms (and the length of the waiting-lists; it was evident that the charismatic renewal and all it involved was what people wanted to come to Whatcombe for. Perhaps it was inevitable that, since the founders of the Barnabas Fellowship had been influenced by the new pentecostalism in the established Churches, Whatcombe was associated in peoples' minds with it.

The majority of our conferences lasted for a weekend or for a midweek period. During the summer months we arranged summer holiday conferences lasting from Saturday to Saturday. Special conferences were arranged at Christmas and Easter (I will describe these in a later chapter).

For about a third of the conferences we invited a guest speaker. Besides enabling our guests to hear Christians with special gifts, this policy was valuable, for it gave the members of the community an opportunity to meet and to listen to someone outside the Fellowship. At first we tended to invite as guest speakers only well-known figures in the charismatic renewal in England, but we gradually broadened this policy to include some who, while not wishing to identify themselves technically as "charismatics", nevertheless were used by the Holy Spirit in charismatic ministries. The experience of working alongside these "non-charismatics" at conferences has been joyfully rewarding.

Reg, Ron and I formed the planning committee. One of us was responsible for the over-all running of a particular conference, but the detailed plans — who was to speak and lead at sessions, who was to be involved in the groups, how special projects were to be organised — were examined by the three of us before being put to the community for final suggestions and approval. If a guest speaker had been invited, the conference leader got in touch with him weeks beforehand to build the programme round his topics and plans.

The application forms indicated the age-group, occupation and denomination of the guests, so it was possible for us to draw up a general picture of the kind of people we could expect at a conference. The applications for a conference on the ministry of the local church, for example, might include a number from clergy, and those for a conference on healing might come largely from people involved in medical care. These were factors we took into account as we planned the programme. If a high proportion of young people had booked for a weekend, we sometimes arranged a barbecue outside for them on the Saturday evening.

The programme for a weekend conference was more intensive than that for a mid-week one. On Friday evening, after dinner, we had a brief introduction to the programme and a service of prayer and praise. On the Saturday morning there were two sessions — the second sometimes taking the form of group discussions — and further groups were arranged after tea if desired. On Saturday evening we had a longer session of prayer and praise together with teaching from one of the community or from the guest speaker. The talks and discussions continued on the Sunday morning, and the conference concluded with a celebration of the eucharist in the afternoon, offering our thanksgiving to God for his blessings during the weekend.

During mid-week conferences there were fewer sessions and the final eucharist was held on Thursday evening. One day, if the weather was fine, one or two of the community took the guests out for a walk and a picnic lunch.

During the conferences members of the community were available for counselling. People asked to see us to discuss all kinds of matters — personal problems, marriage difficulties, guidance over decisions they had to make, spiritual conflicts requiring deliverance, prayer for healing and for renewal in the Holy Spirit. We tried to work in pairs (a man with a woman, not always a husband and wife), but this was not always possible. We left it to individual guests to make the first approach for this — and it was interesting to see how people were led to different members of the community for counselling, not always the ones we might have expected.

To see the Holy Spirit healing and renewing people was — as Reg has said in his Foreword — one of the most rewarding results of our ministry. Various members of the community, especially Reg himself, were particularly gifted in the task of listening to and praying with people who came to them with their problems. There must be dozens if not hundreds of folk whose lives have been transformed in this way. I have seen many who, coming to Whatcombe for the first time with faces drawn with anxiety, have returned the second or third time with eyes lightened with fresh hope.

* * *

What kind of people came to Whatcombe?

Almost all of them were practising Christians, most of them members of established congregations, a few of them members of prayer groups or other communities. Since our ministry was aimed at encouragement within the Church, we did not expect non-Christians to visit us. Evangelistic work through residential conferences was being done by other communities, such as Lee Abbey and Scargill, and we did not wish to duplicate it.

We ran about fifty conferences a year and to them came between one thousand five hundred and two thousand guests. The majority came from London and the South of England — the M3 motorway was opened in 1971 and this brought Whatcombe within two-and-a-half hours' drive of London. A large minority came from the Midlands and the North and some from overseas.

About half of them were members of the Church of England and the other half members of the Free Churches. In the first year we only had one or two Roman Catholics, but the numbers of these have slightly increased, as the charismatic movement touched that Church in this country.*

Most of our guests belonged to those social groups who can afford a second holiday each year or who are prepared to make some personal sacrifice to share in Christian fellowship for a residential week or weekend (although we offered bursaries to those who were unable to afford our fees). To some extent the topic of the conference affected the kind of people who applied to attend, as I have already explained. For example, a conference on ministry to those requiring counselling drew in one doctor, nine nurses, midwives or members of hospital staffs, four school-teachers, one college lecturer, five housewives (all involved in voluntary social work), two youth workers, and an assortment of other men and women in careers varying from secretary to warehouse assistant.

* The first Roman Catholic speaker at Whatcombe came in 1976.

The summer holiday conferences were booked (always with waiting-lists) by people whose main interest was the fellowship offered by the community and its guests combined with relaxation in the countryside or at the sea (it was twenty-five minutes' drive to Lulworth Cove). For Christians who lacked the support of a prayer group in their local churches, the week's holiday was like a spiritual oasis. Nearly all who came in the summer were couples with young children. Looking down the lists of guests I noticed that the fathers' occupations in one week were two school-teachers, one school caretaker, one industrial chemist, one carpenter and joiner, one research engineer, one public relations officer and one accountant. Another week the application forms indicated that we had two clergy, one university professor, one headmaster, three teachers, one industrial engineer, one builder and two clerks.

At certain times of the year we tended to receive many applications from elderly, retired people with the consequence that there was no room for younger people. We therefore adopted a policy of rationing the number of places available to certain age-groups. When we had received ten or a dozen applications from people in their 'sixties and 'seventies, we put further applications from that group on a waiting-list and allocated the remaining places to young people. The result was that most conferences were filled with a widely representative body of folk.

Each conference had a different impact both on the community and on the guests. When the guests arrived the community would almost invariably feel that "this isn't going to be as good as the last one". Looking round at the strange faces in the dining-room and the lounge we would reflect how different they were from our last group! But as the conference unfolded the faces became familiar and each individual became known for his or her gifts and needs. By the final eucharist the unity of Christians in the Body of Christ would be manifest in a new way, and when our guests had departed we would marvel that God had worked afresh among them — and us.

It would be wrong, however, to give the impression that everyone who came to Whatcombe was satisfied with what they found. One priest wrote to us — with tact and kindness — to say that he had been disappointed with the conference he had attended for it had not tackled in depth the subject advertised in our brochure. A young Anglican and his girl-friend left in the middle of another conference saying that our forms of worship were unacceptable to them.

But from the comments we received at the end of conferences and the letters that arrived from guests afterwards, it was evident that many who came returned to their homes, their work and their congregations and prayer groups with a fresh sense of renewal in the Spirit. For some it was, they said, a spiritual turning-point in their lives; for others it was an enlightening and enriching experience; and for the rest it was probably somewhere between those two. In a word of prophecy spoken to us early in 1972, the Lord said, "I will touch everyone who comes to this house." That promise has been fulfilled a countless number of times.

9

WHEN WE WERE parish priests, both Reg and I arranged conferences and holidays for our respective congregations. We took groups to centres for weekends or on holiday trips for a week or a fortnight, and we discovered — as many other clergy have discovered — that these projects brought people together more effectively than almost any other parochial activity. Living, eating, praying, discussing, enjoying ourselves — all under the same roof for a few days — gave us a new experience of what it means to be united in the Body of Christ. The prayer group to which Ron and Jean, Ken and Betty, belonged in Manchester found the same thing. Part of their programme was to spend a weekend together in a hotel or conference centre each year.

Once we began to run conferences at Whatcombe, therefore, we encouraged parish priests and ministers to discuss similar projects with their congregations, offering them free weekends or weeks in our own programme. During the first four years groups came to us from churches all over southern England — Billingshurst,

Blandford, Bournemouth, Farnborough, Horsell, East and West Mersea, Poole, Richmond, Tewkesbury, Tunbridge Wells, Winfarthing, Winton, Woking, Ventnor and Yateley.

The effect of these conferences was always beneficial — to us as a community and (as far as we could tell) to the group that came. What seemed to happen was an encounter, not just between individuals from the congregation and individuals from the community, but between the two groups *as groups*.

What I mean is this. The distinction between a community like the Barnabas Fellowship and a congregation such as that represented by thirty or so members of a local church can be pressed too far. People often refer to "a community" — meaning a residential community — as if it were something totally different from those people whose worship, fellowship, ministry and mission is focused on a church building in the neighbourhood where they live. But, in fact, the two are very similar. The Barnabas Fellowship, like any other community, is but a congregation-in-miniature. Like any local church it is an assembly of Christians; and — again like any local church — its main concern is the worship of Almighty God, the fellowship between its members in the Spirit, and participation in the ministry and mission of Jesus Christ among his people and in his world.

The difference between a community and a congregation is one of structure rather than of kind. Because our fellowship at Whatcombe was more intense than in an average congregation, and because we shared completely in the worship, ministry and mission of our community (rather than in just parts of it, as the ordinary member does in his congregation), we tended to experience the joys and sorrows of Christian discipleship in a more pronounced degree.

The result was that, when a group from a congregation came to stay with us at Whatcombe, they saw in the Fellowship a kind of reflection of themselves — but a reflection in which elements of Christian discipleship were magnified (or maybe distorted!) to an intensity which they had not encountered before.

Take, for example, a churchman's commitment to Christ in terms of the time, the abilities and the money he gives to his local church (the three headings which have become familiar after years of teaching on Christian stewardship). He may well spend several hours each week in activities such as worship, prayer meetings, committees and classes; he may well offer his abilities in various ways — teaching, keeping the accounts, practical work in the church building or in the church hall; he may well give a proportion of his income to the church on a regular weekly or monthly basis.

But when he came to Whatcombe he discovered that he was among another group whose Christian stewardship was exercised in a different way. There the stewardship of time, abilities and money was worked out in terms of a common programme of worship and work each day and a common sharing of possessions and purse. This caused our visitor to think again about his commitment to his congregation in these areas of his personal life.

Or take another aspect of Christian discipleship — the ministry of one member of the Church to another. At

Whatcombe — as in any community — the opportunities we had for ministering to one another were considerable. Hardly a day passed without prayer being offered for one member of the community, and often someone was counselled by another on a personal or spiritual matter. (I have described how we learned to be more open to one another in problems and difficulties.) Consequently, we were used to giving or receiving help from one another in prayer, listening, counselling, laying on of hands, sacrament, and so on.

When a group from a congregation came to stay with us, they sensed the mutual support that the members of the Barnabas Fellowship gave one another. They noticed how we related to one another in the dozens of little things that make up Christian discipleship in living, praying and working together. And the fact that we represented different Christian traditions made this unity in the Fellowship all the more remarkable.

Now I am not suggesting that we exercised a "higher" form of Christian stewardship at Whatcombe or that we discovered a "deeper" degree of unity (whatever those expressions might mean!). One does not lose selfishness or self-centredness just by belonging to a community! But because we were forced to face the causes of our personal weaknesses among ourselves and seek God's grace to overcome them — especially in these areas of stewardship and unity — our guests saw that the Lord was triumphing over them and this gave them encouragement to face their own personal weaknesses in their own congregation.

Nor am I suggesting that the blessing was all one-way! When a group from a parish or a congregation visited us, the community benefited, too. The opportunity of sharing our life and home with others who were responding corporately to the call of Jesus Christ in circumstances very different from our own was an inspiring and challenging experience for us as well. Our guests were engaged in the mission of Jesus Christ in the world on a greater scale than we were. They were maintaining the fellowship and ministry of the Church against far greater difficulties than we encountered. To hear of the ways in which the Lord was working through them was encouraging indeed, and it was with a sense of being the privileged ones that we welcomed them at Whatcombe.

The truth is that, in meeting each other — congregation and community — we were each blessed. This experience of being built up by one another is echoed exactly in Paul's words to the church in Rome: "I long to see you, that I may impart to you some spiritual gift to strengthen you, that is, that we may be mutually encouraged by each other's faith, both yours and mine" (Romans 1: 11–12). Just as individual Christians can help each other through the spiritual gifts that God gives them individually, so can groups of God's people help each other through the gifts that the Spirit brings to them corporately as well.

Thanksgiving to God for his goodness to us, community as well as guests, often overflowed in a moving way during the final eucharist of these conferences. For me, one of the joys was to be able to preside over a celebration of the eucharist in the lounge or in the chapel with the members of the community mingled among the guests. I have already explained how our worship evolved in such a way that creativity and spontaneity sprang out of the order we adopted. On such occasions the members of the community were a highly gifted team of worship-leaders, ready for anything to which the Spirit might lead them — a prayer, a chorus, a dance-movement, singing in the spirit, a prophecy, speaking in tongues, an interpretation, an inspired picture, a passage of scripture, a visual aid. Together we moved through the structure of the service with a relaxed orderliness and freedom that was like the movement of the water in a stream flowing smoothly between the banks that directed its course.

Our guests were nearly always caught up into this powerful spirit of thanksgiving and praise. Occasionally one or two felt uncomfortable or threatened by the experience, but for the majority it opened up wider prospects of what it means to worship in the Spirit, using the form and the texts of a service which was (for the Anglicans among them, at any rate) familiar. Staid churchwardens embraced others in the congregation during the giving of the Peace with a warmth and friendliness that they would have found difficult to express in a parish church. Ordinary communicants passed the paten and chalice round among themselves and administered the sacrament to one another in a manner that might have shocked them if they had been invited to do this at the altar rail. When the group returned to their local church, they nearly always went back to their regular worship with a new sense of liberation and a fresh expectancy after being with us.

* * *

What other effects did these conferences have on the groups that came to us — and, more importantly, on the congregations they represented?

It is impossible to answer that question, even in general terms. Judging by the letters we received after they had returned home, some of them seem to have been helped a good deal. An Anglican vicar wrote to us after a weekend to say that everyone whom he had brought to Whatcombe had been blessed in one way or another. A United Reformed minister wrote to say that, in his estimation, the conference had been the beginning of a new chapter in his church's ministry to the neighbourhood. (On the other hand, a curate who had brought a group of young people told me some months afterwards that he had been disappointed — although in fairness I should say that he had imagined bringing them to a holiday party rather than to a weekend of talks, discussions and worship!)

But it was in the building up of relationships between individuals in the congregations and in helping them to discover what the Lord could do in them and through them as they grew in unity with each other that perhaps the most important effects were to be found.

This was particularly so in the case of clergy-congregation relationships. Often a vicar or a minister and his flock would come to know and trust and respect one another in a new way after spending a weekend at Whatcombe.

In one instance these relationships were transformed. We had welcomed a group from a parish with a new vicar, who came with them to Whatcombe. He had returned after working overseas for many years. Having been used to acting in a strongly paternalistic fashion — saying what was to be done in congregations and how money was to be spent — he soon found himself at odds with his English flock. While it would be inaccurate to say that they disliked him, it was certainly true that when they came to us there was a gulf fixed between this priest and the rest of the group.

During the course of the weekend, both he and the group came to realise the need for reconciliation between themselves. (In one of the talks we had told them something of the difficulties we had experienced as a community.) After the final eucharist on the Sunday afternoon, they remained by themselves in the lounge for over an hour. We never learned what happened, but God brought the priest and the group together in a wonderful manner during that time, and this reconciliation affected the whole congregation of that parish.

The links we built up with parishes and congregations through these conferences led us to consider other ways in which we could make ourselves available to those who visited us. In some cases one or two members of the community went to the local church before the conference to meet the people who had booked to attend and to plan with them the programme for their weekend at Whatcombe. This preliminary visit gave the group from the congregation an opportunity to meet members of the Barnabas Fellowship so that when they eventually came to us they felt more at home. It also helped the vicar or the minister organising the conference to persuade waverers to make up their minds about joining in. (When the waverers saw that the community members were fairly normal human beings, they usually signed their application forms and paid their booking fees!)

Months after the conference we made a return visit to the local church to meet the group again and to speak to the whole congregation at a public meeting or at a service in church. This was a chance for the group to consult us on any problems that had cropped up since the conference. Quite often, after a congregational conference at Whatcombe, prayer groups were formed and, by the time of this return visit by members of the community, they needed help in sorting out early difficulties or advice on the way in which their ministry was to develop.

These preliminary and return visits to local congregations became part of a growing ministry of outreach that took most of us away from Whatcombe for two or three weeks each year. Besides running conferences in the house, we now found ourselves invited to all parts of the British Isles.

But the account of this development deserves a chapter on its own . . .

10

AMONG THE PEOPLE who came to Whatcombe were clergy and other responsible churchmen who were experiencing renewal in their congregations and prayer groups. As the charismatic movement spread through the churches in Britain in the 'seventies, an increasing number of people rang us up and asked if they could come and talk to us about the implication of renewal for their congregations and about the problems that it raised.

So it was that we found ourselves being used as a consultative centre for all kinds of matters in the area of renewal: the pastoral care of those who have been baptised in the Spirit, the formation and maintenance of charismatic prayer groups, the training of group leaders, the exercise of the gifts of the Spirit within the context of ordinary church worship and ministry, healing and deliverance. We were also approached by Christians who were planning the establishment of new communities or who were members of communities that were experiencing problems.

Out of these consultations came many invitations to speak at gatherings throughout the British Isles—and beyond. Like most of the things that developed out of our life and ministry together, these invitations created problems for us! Naturally, we wanted to accept as many of these as we could. The Lord often used occasions like these powerfully, and our presence at big meetings in different parts of the country advertised the community's existence and ministry.

But the absence of two or more community members during a conference threw additional work on those who remained at Whatcombe, so we usually went away only out of conference time. Individually we always consulted the rest of the Fellowship before we accepted an engagement that took us away for more than a day. This was a good discipline. It helped us to discern the relative value of one kind of invitation compared with another, and it meant that when we were away the rest of the community felt that they were involved in what we did. If I was away for more than a few days, I made a point of ringing them up or writing to them to tell them how I was getting on.

Several parishes invited two or three of us for what might be called "weekends of renewal". The purpose and pattern of these weekends varied, but our experience in one might be taken as typical. The vicar and a number of his congregation had been baptised in the Spirit and they were seeking to bring the strength and joy of renewal to the rest of the congregation without creating a division among them.

Months before the weekend, we advised the vicar on the formation of a number of prayer groups and provided him with scripture studies and literature that would help them seek the Lord's guidance in their ministry within that congregation. We also showed him how these groups formed a sub-structure to the existing congregation and were not separate from it.

When the weekend arrived, the members of the community met the group leaders on the Friday night. Part of the evening consisted of a question-and-answer session (they had things they wanted to discuss with us, mostly to do with the topics I have just listed); for the rest of the time we led them in prayer and praise as a model of the kind of devotion they might encourage in their groups.

On the Saturday afternoon and evening an extended public meeting, with a tea interval, was organised in the church hall. We spoke about renewal in the Spirit, and the evening ended with an informal service of praise, led by a guitar group. The purpose of this meeting was to open up the subject to the congregation and to anyone in the neighbourhood who was interested. We preached in church at the Sunday services and then, during the next two days, spent time with each of the prayer groups. Sometimes other meetings were arranged—with the local ministers' fraternal or similar associations.

Weekends such as these were certainly encouraging to the members of the community who took part in them. They enabled us to keep in touch with the renewal movement in parishes and congregations and they helped us to shape our teaching in conferences at Whatcombe when individuals or groups from other churches came seeking guidance in the opportunities and problems that confronted them.

* * *

From the first days when we arrived at Whatcombe, we were welcomed into the company of other communites, old as well as new. I have already described how some of the Lee Abbey community came to a retreat at the beginning of 1972. Since then we have exchanged numerous visits with that community and with the International Students' Club in London. Various members of the Scargill community came to our conferences. We also had close contacts with Fellowship House near Brentwood after Chris Hill and his wife, Lindy, went there. Chris and Lindy were frequent visitors to Whatcombe when he had been on the staff of a Poole parish.

It was during our first years that Sir Thomas and Lady Lees began to establish a community at Post Green, about ten miles away, based on a number of extended households in the Lytchett Minster district. Reg and Lucia had become friends of Tom and Faith in the 'sixties when Post Green was a centre for renewal in the South of England, drawing together a team of gifted teachers from different Christian traditions. We saw this team develop into a community with wide outreach, supported by a ministry of cassettes and pamphlets which they produced themselves.

Also near us was Hilfield, the headquarters of the Anglican Society of St. Francis. The brothers from there occasionally joined in the Sunday afternoon eucharists at Whatcombe and invited us to various events in their life. The prior of a large Roman Catholic monastery came to see us a number of times, interested in our form of mixed community. One or two nuns appeared on some of our lists of conference guests, sent by their sisters in religion to learn more about us! One sister, dispatched by her mother superior to investigate "that pentecostalist place in Dorset", was baptised in the Spirit with considerable personal release during the conference: she went back to her convent rejoicing but wondering how she was going to account for what had happened when she saw "mother"! A mother superior came specifically for the laying on of hands for baptism in the Spirit and left praising God for his goodness to her.

I was invited to the conference of the Anglican Religious Communities held in York in July 1974 to address the three hundred participants on the subject of "Community and the Pentecostal Experience". After describing the renewal movement and the origins, life and ministry of the Barnabas Fellowship, I drew a comparison between Whatcombe and the communities represented at the conference:

"If there is any justification in calling the Barnabas Fellowship a 'charismatic community', it is perhaps that we do not look back to any founder or rule as the basis of our life and worship like many of you do. Rather, we seek the immediate power and guidance of God the Holy Spirit to shape our fellowship and to lead our activities, believing that he will make his will known to us and that he will equip us through his charisms to fulfil that will.

'But as we do this, we find that our fellowship and our activities have a close kinship with the lives and the ministries of the older religious communities, and that we can look to them for guidance. For it is the same Lord who has guided and equipped his people in the past. God still speaks to us through the Rule of St. Benedict and the example of St. Francis. The authentic tradition of the Church never quenches the Spirit. It acts as a signpost to what God can do in our day if we commit ourselves to him in Jesus Christ as our forefathers in the faith did. All of us who follow the Spirit in this way are charismatics."

On the last night, after Compline in the spacious modern chapel of St. John's College, York, sixty or so religious stayed behind for prayer and praise, seated on the carpet round the free-standing altar. Two members of the community of the Sisters of the Church, Ham Common, led the singing with guitars. We ministered to one another in tiny groups of three or four. One nun was baptised in the Spirit. Two sisters prayed for me with the laying on of hands. We remained together until well after midnight. It was one of the most thrilling events I have ever attended, for it demonstrated how the renewal movement is bringing fresh faith and hope and joy to the traditional communites in the Anglican Communion.

* * *

But the excursions from Whatcombe that moved me most were the three trips I made — one with Reg, another with my wife — to visit charismatic groups in Ireland.

Early in 1973 I received a letter from the Rev. Cecil Kerr, then chaplain of the Queen's University, Belfast, inviting me to share in number of renewal meetings that spring. The Fellowship decided without hesitation that I should go.

That first trip to Belfast was a never-to-be-forgotten experience. On the one hand there was the grim reality behind the pictures I had seen on the TV news programme — the ruined buildings, the broken and boarded windows, the barriers, the security forces, and armoured cars and the so-called "peace line" (a high corrugated-iron wall separating the two areas of the city). On the other hand there were the obvious signs of God's love among the groups of Christians that I met — groups that included Roman Catholics as well as Protestants.

During the months before my visit, Cecil had found himself increasingly involved in the charismatic movement as he and a number of his friends experienced the renewing power of the Holy Spirit in their lives. He was astonished to find himself sensing a new unity, not only with Presbyterians, Methodists and other Protestants, but also with Roman Catholics who were being touched by the Holy Spirit. As an Irish Anglican he had been used to debating with Roman Catholics; he had not been used to praying with them and loving them! He discovered that charismatic prayer groups, consisting of Protestants and Roman Catholics, were springing up not only in Northern Ireland but also in the Republic, and he arranged a weekend conference for some of them in Belfast. It was to this that I was invited.

At one large meeting I heard Protestants and Roman Catholics explain how their former suspicion and hostility for one another had been dissolved and replaced by a growing love and understanding. A young seminarian revealed how his strong Republican ideas combined with a bitter anti-British hatred had melted. A Jesuit confessed that he had never been north of the Border until he had been invited to attend the conference, and that the fear he had in his heart at the prospect of the journey had been removed and exchanged for a sense of wonder at the love he had experienced.

A Presbyterian deaconess described how, in a prayer group she attended, a young Protestant girl who had lost a close relative at the hands of the IRA was embraced by a Catholic girl whose brother had been killed the previous week by extremists. A pastor from an Evangelical church confessed that it was the first time he had ever spoken to Catholic nuns and that he was astonished to discover what real Christians they were.

On the Sunday of the conference, Cecil presided at an ecumenical eucharist in the chaplaincy church. For the giving of the Peace and the receiving of the sacrament, a hundred and fifty of us formed a large circle round the free-standing altar. As I looked round during the singing of "We are one in the Spirit", I recognised members of every major Christian denomination — including Roman Catholics (priests and religious as well as laity). I could hardly believe such a thing was possible in the heart of Belfast.

During this visit and in the next two I was able to visit other groups in Dublin, Waterford and Cork; but nothing, I think, will ever equal the wonder I felt at that first Belfast charismatic conference: in the midst of destruction and death the Holy Spirit was re-establishing the people of God in the unity they already possessed in Jesus Christ. To describe it Cecil quoted his own version of Ephesians 2: 13 (in *Today's English Version*):

> We who used to be far away have been brought near by the death of Christ. For Christ himself has brought

us peace, by making the Catholics and the Protestants one people. With his own body he broke down the wall that separated us and kept us apart . . . By his death on the cross Christ destroyed the hatred; by means of the cross he united both in a single body and brought them back to God.

Cecil and his wife, Myrtle, told me that they believed the Lord would one day call them to form a community which would demonstrate within its membership how Irish Protestants and Roman Catholics can live, worship and work together in the power of the Holy Spirit. Later that year Cecil spent a few days at Whatcombe discussing the project with us.

In 1974 the Kerrs moved to Glenmore, a large house on the road along the northern shore of Carlingford Lough near Rostrevor, and a number of Christians joined them to live together. The story of the establishment of this Christain Renewal Centre is as remarkable as the story of the beginnings at Whatcombe — the same faith-testing, uncertainties in the early stages, the same miraculous response to prayers, the same joys and sorrows, anxieties and victories. Towards the end of that year Margaret and I spent a week with them, sharing in the ministry of their groups and conferences and discussing with them the problems of community living.

One evening we walked up the hill behind Glenmore — the Mountains of Mourne rise behind Rostrevor — until we reached a point where we could look out southwards over the lough. The water is about two miles across at this point. To the left the lough widens to join the Irish

Sea; to the right it narrows into a river. On the opposite shore is the Irish Republic.

It was getting dark, and two lines of road lights stretched out like sparkling necklaces in front of us. One ran along the road below, following the shore road of the lough to our right; the other ran along the road on the opposite shore of the lough; both converged in the far distance where the waters of the lough narrowed to a river and the border between the Republic and Northern Ireland began. The Renewal Centre was established to do just that, we both thought — to bring together the lights of Christian ministry and mission represented by the two great religious and cultural traditions which are the heritage of those who live north and south of the Border.

* * *

In these journeyings we were always aware of the prayer and support of the community. When I stood up to address an audience, I felt that it was the Barnabas Fellowship that spoke through me by the unity and inspiration of the Spirit: this gave me a confidence and an authority that was unlike anything I had experienced before. When Paul said that he was present with the church in Corinth "in spirit", he was not using a pious platitude: he was expressing a spiritual reality.

I had a practical demonstration of this solidarity on one occasion when, during a visit to a college, I was asked to lead a group of students in prayer. I had had a busy few days and I was extremely tired. The time was twenty minutes to three in the afternoon — I remember looking at my watch and calculating how long it would be before I could slip away and get back to Whatcombe!

Then, quite unexpectedly, I was suddenly aware of an in-filling of the Holy Spirit. My tiredness vanished and a new eagerness and sense of expectancy welled up within me. The prayers with that group lasted until after four o'clock and, as far as I could discern, were a blessing to many of those who were there.

When I got back to Whatcombe that night, one of the Fellowship asked me casually, "Was everything all right today?"

"Why?" I asked.

"Because this afternoon — as some of us were decorating a bedroom — we felt we ought to stop work and pray for you."

"And did you?"

"Of course!"

"What time was that?" I asked, yet knowing what I would be told.

"We hadn't been back long after lunch — just after half past two, I believe."

11

Celebrations are important in any family: they are not less so in a community. The Church's liturgical festivals provided us with opportunities for rejoicing in the great events of God's saving work in Jesus Christ with our guests, and the birthdays and wedding anniversaries gave us a chance to enjoy ourselves as a community.

Holy Week and Easter have always occupied a special place in my interest and affection. As a student of Christian liturgy, the ancient observances have had an absorbing fascination for me. The Easters that I spent at Whatcombe — when we adapted the traditional ceremonies to our domestic setting — are, therefore, precious memories.

The Easter conference began on the Wednesday in Holy Week and finished on the Monday after Easter Day. On the evening of Maundry Thursday we celebrated the eucharist within the context of a supper (which we called a "Christian Passover"). Lucia and Margaret Bradley prepared a menu of cold lamb, salad, matzos bread and figs, and the scripture reading, the prayers and the Communion took place during this meal.

Our observance of Good Friday varied. Once we took guests on a procession round the grounds at various positions or "stations" where we had set up pictures of Christ's Passion. Another year we kept a two hours' vigil with prayers, hymns and dramatic readings.

On Easter Eve we adapted the ceremonies of the traditional service — the blessing of the paschal candle, the reading of the prophecies of the resurrection and the reaffirmation of our baptismal promises — to a time of prayer and praise in our lounge. We arranged the chairs in a wide circle and in the middle of the room placed a large metal bowl of water, about three feet in diameter, decorated round the edges with moss and primroses. A younger member of the community fixed a large candle to a stand in

the middle of the water and by its flickering light we listened to the readings, prayed, and committed ourselves afresh to the risen Lord.

On Easter Day we celebrated the eucharist in the lounge with the sun streaming through the high windows and the first signs of spring appearing on the trees outside. We had always hoped that it would be possible for us to do this out-of-doors, but during the time I was at Whatcombe the weather was never kind enough. (At the back of the house was a fine old avenue of tall trees that looked like nature's cathedral!)

The weekend of the feast of Pentecost and harvest-time in September were marked by special conferences on these themes; but it was at Christmas that the Christian celebration gave us some wonderful days at Whatcombe.

About half our visitors were members of our own families — parents, brothers and sisters with their children — and the rest were friends and folk who had written in to book a place at the house-party advertised in our brochure. It was not a conference in the formal sense of the word; rather, it was an occasion when all of us — the fifty or so in the house — rejoiced in the birth of the Saviour of mankind and celebrated in an appropriate manner the joy of being together.

Preparations began weeks before. The ladies commandeered the dining-room as a place where decorations could be made (their ingenuity seemed boundless) and presents wrapped. The men sawed up logs for the fire in the library. I went to a neighbouring estate with Mark, Catherine and Jonathan to receive the gift of a huge Christmas tree, which the young people decorated.

The guests arrived on Christmas Eve. In the evening we posed scenes from the Nativity, using the main staircase as a stage, and sang carols by candlelight. On Christmas morning we woke our guests up by singing carols outside their bedrooms. After breakfast the eucharist was celebrated in the lounge, and at tea-time we met in the library for Father Christmas's visit. (Ray the first two years, Trevor the next two—arriving mysteriously up the drive on the community's baby tractor, to the excited delight of the younger guests!) Dinner was eaten in the evening.

The following days provided a varied programme—Bible studies in the morning, walks in the afternoon, and in the evening play-reading, stories round the library fire, folk dancing and workshops in which people tested their literary and artistic skills.

The great house came to life during this festival. Walking up the drive we could see the decorated Christmas tree with its fairy lights sparkling through the library window. Children in their best clothes laughed and played in the entrance hall as we went in, and the happy atmosphere of the place enveloped us like a cloak. When I was young I envied the experiences that Mr. Pickwick and his followers had when they spent Christmas at Dingley Dell. How I wished I could spend Christmases like that! A Whatcombe Christmas was similar to the festival Charles Dickens portrayed—but so much better, for its spirit of enjoyment sprang from a living faith in what God had done in Jesus Christ for mankind.

* * *

In the midst of running conferences and going out to fulfil speaking engagements, we were often so busy that we hardly had time to enjoy one another's company. This was a grave weakness, for unless the members of a community can relax together as well as work and pray together, their growth into unity is seriously impeded. Prayer, work and recreation — the older religious communities, looking back to the wisdom of St. Benedict, knew the importance of this third element in their lives. We had become so used to labouring long hours together that at one stage we almost felt guilty if we lazed in the sun or sat round the fire in the library talking.

Fortunately, we learned the lesson of relaxing together in time. On a summer's day, when the last of the guests had departed, we would pack a box of food, bundle swimming-costumes and towels into a bag, and drive down to the coast for a beach picnic. Sometimes a friend of the community would send us a generous cheque with instructions that we were to go out and treat ourselves to a meal. We had favourite haunts where we could fulfil instructions like these! — a hotel whose picture-windows overlooked Swanage bay, a village pub where we could serve ourselves from about thirty dishes and sit by an open log fire, and a restaurant by a quay where, after dinner, we could stroll along the riverbank in the twilight towards Poole harbour. Then there were the visits to the theatre, the cinema and concert-hall when the members of the community occupied a whole row of seats and consumed large quantities of ice-cream!

Times of recreation like these reminded us that the Lord had brought us together *to be a community.* It was easy to forget that in a busy conference season. True, as a Fellowship, we had a ministry to fulfil among our fellow-Christians in the Church! But we were not to be just a group of people who ran a conference centre. We were to be a family in the Family of God.

We discovered that, relaxing together as well as praying together!

* * *

One evening a group of theological college students arrived for a conference. They had heard stories about us and some of them were not sure what to expect. When they came into the library, they saw Reg sitting on the floor playing a game of miniature football with Mark. He greeted them cheerily and then went on with the game. Two days later, just before they went back to college, they said that what had helped them to feel at home from the beginning was the sight of the warden playing with his son. They realised that they had not come to some high-powered institution; they had come into a family.

This was one of the great contributions made by Mark, Catherine and Jonathan to our communal life. Their presence among us — dashing off to school, messing about in the kitchen and in the workshop, playing tennis, joining us on our excursions — helped us to be more *human* in our attitude. Without them, it would have been less easy to find reasons of relaxation.

Mark, Catherine and Jonathan were the children of community members most affected by our life together. Jeffrey Dodgson was only with us during his holidays in the first year, and Elizabeth East was away at school and then in nurse training.

Before they had come to Whatcombe, their parents had asked them if they were happy about the move, and they had all said yes. Initially they were as enthusiastic as the rest of us. But as the months went by, all three of them — like the rest of us — sensed the strains of community living from time to time. Since their parents were often busy when they were home from school — in the evenings and at weekends — they were sometimes disappointed that the family could not watch the television or do other things together as often as in an ordinary home.

To compensate for this, Reg and Lucia, and Ken and Betty, made special efforts to spend time with their children when they were free — on days off and during evenings and weekends when there were no conferences. Or, when the parents were otherwise engaged, another member of the community would spend an evening with the children or take them out on a treat.

Mark, Catherine and Jonathan had been used to living in ordinary urban roads with friends in nearby houses, and Whatcombe's comparative isolation was a big change for them. There was some compensation in having the countryside to explore together, a baby tractor to drive, and unlimited use of the house's facilities, but it was not the same as their lives had been in Mersea and Manchester.

However, as they grew older, they were drawn — by their own choice — more into the community's ministry. Mark and Jonathan played musical instruments (piano, violin, horn, guitars) at our gatherings; Catherine assisted in the cooking and waiting at table. They came to conference sessions and took part in dramatic presentations. On one memorable occasion Reg and Lucia quizzed Mark and Catherine during a session on Christian family life about their experience of being brought up in the East household. The two young people spoke frankly and lovingly, showing that they appreciated the problems they had caused their parents. It was clear to the guests who listened that their affection and gratitude for Reg and Lucia was deep and genuine. That session indicated that, whatever else Whatcombe had done, it had strengthened and matured the relationships between the young people and their families.

12

For the nine or ten of us living at Whatcombe, there was always the danger of exclusiveness. It would have been easy for us to have become inward-looking and detached, out of touch with the flow of society around us.

The Lord saved us from this, I think, by two things. One was the ministry to which he called us, involving us as it did with an increasingly large number of people in all parts of the country. Our contact with them did not end when they drove away down the road after a conference. Through visits, letters and telephone calls, we became involved in their lives, their problems, their prayer groups and their congregations. We could not be out of touch with the flow of society around us when we were in touch with so many people within that society.

The other was the self-examination to which the Lord subjected us at intervals. We were always having to turn to God for grace and guidance in our community life, and our awareness of this need meant that we often had to look beyond ourselves for the help of others.

This help came in varying ways—from guests, from

visiting speakers, from friends, from members of churches in our neighbourhood. Most of them never knew what their friendship, their advice and their prayers meant to us. They kept us in contact with what seemed to us normality when our experiences were anything but normal!

But we were particularly grateful for a number of wise men and women who seem to have been sent by God to Whatcombe at crucial moments to minister to us as a community.

We were visited one day in 1973 by a travelling evangelist from India, Brother Barnabas. He was introduced to us by a nearby clergyman and we were so impressed that we asked him to return the next day and spend it with us. Through a remarkable gift of prophetic insight, Brother Barnabas revealed to us those weaknesses which were damaging our corporate life. After he had departed, we felt we had been washed clean and encouraged by an apostolic visitation.

The Rev. Graham Pulkingham spent a week with us in 1974. Formerly rector of the Church of the Redeemer, Houston, Texas, and now a member of the Community of Celebration in this country, he observed our activities and then spent a long afternoon with us, making suggestions about the manner in which pastoral leadership was exercised in our Fellowship and about the re-structuring of our lives so that the single members were "adopted" into families (a policy I explained earlier).

The following year our community retreat was conducted by Canon Geoffrey Paul, Warden of Lee Abbey. He gave us a wider vision of the Spirit's activity in the world, in the Church, and in the Christian community, and took the rôle of a consultant during a day's discussions on what we experienced at Whatcombe.

These visitors and others (and their wives) helped us to realise what a healthy exercise it is for any community to open itself from time to time to the inspection and advice of sympathetic but detached observers. In the older religious communities this ministry was fulfilled by an individual know technically as "the Visitor" (usually the bishop of the diocese or the superior of another community). Our "Visitors" were more informal but no less Spirit-led.

* * *

As we became more open to spiritual gifts such as a word of prophecy or an interpretation of a tongue in our community prayers, we found the Lord encouraging us or checking us through these charisms.

I can recall three occasions when his word came to us in ways that moved us deeply.

The first occurred soon after we had opened Whatcombe as a conference centre. One of the community was given a word of wisdom during prayers: "I shall minister to others through you as you minister to one another."

When I heard this, I was inclined to dismiss it as dangerous advice. Surely we would become introspective and cliquish if we paid more attention to one another than to our guests? But slowly we realised the truth of this word of wisdom. We saw that it *was* as we cared more for each other in the community that the love of Christ overflowed, as it were, from us to our guests.

Had I looked more discerningly at the scriptures I

would have found that truth there! "By this will all men know that you are my disciples, if you have love for one another," said the Christ of the Fourth Gospel (John 13: 35). "May the Lord make you increase and abound in love to each other and to all men," Paul prayed for one of his congregations (I Thessalonians 3: 12) — that is, begin by loving those closest to them in the Christian family ("one another") and then that love will spill out towards others ("all men").

The second instance was a picture which came into my mind one day during prayers — a "simple vision" as it is called in neo-pentecostal circles. I described it to the rest of the community.

What I saw were the pieces of a jigsaw puzzle coming together and making a complete picture which I knew represented the Barnabas Fellowship. But as I looked at it, the jigsaw was broken up again. Then I noticed that the pieces were in the shape of human beings — the members of the community — and that the picture had broken up because the "pieces" were all growing and changing their shape. The process of putting them together to re-form the picture had to begin all over again.

The simple vision gave us an insight into why it was that relationships within the Fellowship were never on an even keel for any length of time. So often we seemed to reach a stage of mutual understanding and harmony with one another, and then something would happen to spoil the unity. We now realised that none of us is static like the pieces of a real jigsaw puzzle. As we grow nearer to Christ (or as we move away from him), our "shapes" change, and we have to learn to live together as each individual member comes through these changes. Unity was a goal we should be moving towards in the Spirit; it was not something we could achieve perfectly in this life.

The third instance was a prophetic utterance in the form of six questions. The charism was exercised through Rosemary — and this was all the more remarkable, for Rosemary did not often say much during community prayers.

One morning, during a period of silence, she said suddenly, "I believe the Lord is going to speak to us."

Fortunately, Reg had a pencil and paper in his hand at that moment, and he wrote the questions down as she spoke them — slowly and with an authority that was not hers:

Who am I?

Who are you and why are you here?

Who or what is the most important thing in your life at this very hour?

Whose house is this?

Why do you wish people to come here — for your own sakes, or for their sake, or for my sake?

Do you love me?

The questions were so direct that they had a stunning effect on us when we first heard them. Reg wisely suggested that we thought about them and discussed them at some future date. We typed them out and put the slips of paper in our Bibles. We often returned to them during the next two years. They compelled our attention and searched out our hidden motives.

Who am I? We had to look beyond ourselves and our concerns to Almighty God himself: "I am that I am." If we were concerned about paying our bills or if we became argumentative over a detail in the programme, those three words were like a trumpet-call, summoning us to stand to attention and to look upwards. God *is*. He is in everything. All circumstances, all problems, are in his hands. That was the faith on which we were to act.

Who are you and why are you here? For some of us there was always a temptation to try and make Whatcombe a success by our own efforts so that people would wonder at what *we* had done rather than what the Lord was doing through us (and in spite of us!). This question forced us to reset our spiritual compasses when we planned any new project or policy: were we doing this for the Lord?

Who or what is the most important thing in your life at this very hour? Any one of us could slip into self-righteousness or self-pity when it seemed as if the pressures of community living were overpowering us. The old Adam was ready to raise himself up in us if we turned our eyes away from Christ. When I was feeling depressed or impatient with the rest of the community, this question was a saving reminder that Jesus Christ and his will for me was to be the focus of my attention. I had no rights for myself; my only right was what Jesus gave me.

Whose house is this? It was fortunate that we rented Whatcombe. This prevented us from being too possessive about it as a piece of property. It was the house that God had led us to in order that we could minister in the name of Jesus Christ. Because the building belonged to Patricia Chichester, we could never think of it as ours.

Why do you wish people to come — for your sake, or for their sakes, or for my sake? If we looked at our own interests in running conferences, we would have been like a business enterprise with religion thrown in. If we had looked only at the interests of our guests, then we might have modified our policies and our programmes to attract the largest number of appreciative visitors. But by remembering why God had brought us to Whatcombe, we were helped to look beyond these concerns to the ministry in which we were engaged within the work of the whole Church of Christ.

Do you love me? The question that the risen Lord addressed to Peter before he charged the apostle with his pastoral ministry was addressed to us, too. Unless all we did sprang from the love we had for God, then we were but a noisy gong or a clanging cymbal, whatever spiritual gifts were manifested through us for the renewal of the Church.

It was vital that we should be discerning where the love of God was taking us — as individuals as well as a community. We were not called to Whatcombe to please ourselves or anyone else — not even the other members of the Fellowship.

I would stress this last point. Because we are members of a community, we cannot abrogate our personal responsibility as individual Christians before God. In some circles where the charismatic renewal has brought into being new forms of communal life, there is a view that the Christian should identify his submission to Jesus Christ with his submission to the Church as manifested in the community to which he belongs.

This, I believe, is a dangerous doctrine. The truth it

contains is that we must be prepared to lay our lives down for one another within the Christian fellowship and submit to the authority of those raised up to lead that fellowship. The error it admits is that any group of Christians will be led infallibly by the Spirit at all times and in all circumstances.

The forces which influence the decision-making processes of the most charismatic community will not always be sent from heaven. Just as sinless perfection is beyond the hope of any Christian in this world, so freedom from error is beyond the certainty of any Christian group.

So the individual must test what he feels he must do as a member of the group with what he believes is the will of God for him. There will be times when he will feel in rebellion against the rest. Nearly always he will learn that his rebellion comes from his own lack of humility, his own unwillingness to submit to what God is saying to him through his brothers and sisters in Christ. But there may also be occasions when his rebellion is not motivated by a sinful tendency within himself but by the Holy Spirit, who is using him to prevent the community from making a mistake. Then he becomes the prophet within the fellowship, to proclaim the will of God to the others that the life of Jesus might be glorified among them.

I can think of several instances where one or two members of the Barnabas Fellowship persistently opposed ideas and suggestions until at length the rest of us came to see that what they said was right and wise. Opposition of this kind requires gifts of discernment and steadfastness — discernment to recognise the voice of God amidst the human inclinations, steadfastness to resist the mounting pressure from the rest of the group who can — often quite unconsciously — make the individual who is opposing them feel rejected and lonely in their midst.

* * *

I can sum up my experience of community in the beginnings at Whatcombe by saying that it was for me a classroom, a sanctuary and a home — all in one.

The community was a classroom for it was there that I learned more about myself and about others than I had ever done before. We can only know ourselves through the fellowship of others. Only when we can see the effect we have on other people do we come to know ourselves more clearly. Even people who have lived with husband or wife or children discover things about themselves which they did not know before when they enter the wider family of a community and see the reactions of the other members to themselves.

This can be a hurtful revelation, for we do not like to be confronted with the results of our own weaknesses. But it can be a comforting and encouraging one, too, for others notice more quickly than we do when the Spirit of God is beginning to melt, mould, fill and strengthen us.

The same thing happens in our relationship with the rest of the community. As we discover attitudes or habits in them that repel us, we also find that the Lord gently teaches us to love them in spite of what we feel about them. Then we notice one day that what once repelled us has disappeared. He has changed them, too.

The community was a sanctuary because it was there that I saw God glorified. During the early months, when we were preparing the house, we thought of ourselves as a community and, in a sense, we were. But it was only a shallow form of community. When we turned to our ministry of running conferences, it was evident that our unity was not strong enough to bear the strains that that ministry made on us, and we had to submit in penitence to the Holy Spirit and allow him to bring us into a new unity by his power.

So we learned that community is a by-product of the Spirit. Our setting out to create community did not bring it into being. The Lord had to do that for us. This is how it was in the New Testament. The apostles did not discuss how they were to form the Church. When the Holy Spirit came, the community was created among them.

It follows from this that community is not ultimately dependent upon any technique or structure. We assembled at Whatcombe with little idea of what being a community meant. Although this ignorance caused us to make many mistakes, it also meant that in the end we saw the Spirit at work creating a community among us.

The community was also a home for me because it was there that I found a loving acceptance among the other members of the Fellowship. I took the welcoming attitude of the community towards me for granted at first. Only slowly did it dawn on me that their courtesy, encouragement, sharing, listening, caring — with all the little acts of kindness that brighten up each day — were mine because the others were putting me before themselves. So it was that at Whatcombe I learned how the great New Testament themes of fellowship and service merge with one another in a truly Spirit-filled community.

Epilogue

My wife and I left Whatcombe in November 1975. The Lord had shown us the next stage of our personal pilgrimage and, after much discussion and prayer with the community, we made plans to go.

It was, if anything, more difficult to leave the Barnabas Fellowship than it had been to decide to join. Of course, Margaret and I had things to look forward to — a home of our own, new people to meet, a fascinating ministry to fulfil.

Nevertheless, those last days with the community are poignant memories. We spent an evening with each family in turn. We shared in a sumptuous farewell dinner. Just before our departure, we knelt to receive the laying on of hands in blessing from the Fellowship at the end of a eucharist in the chapel.

And as we drove through the familiar gates for the last time, we slowed the car down in the lane to Winterborne Whitechurch to look back. Across the fields, the great house stood square and grey among trees that were gold and dark in the morning sunshine. We saw a tiny figure move in the yard at the back of Whatcombe: Ken Taylor was collecting logs for the library fire.

We felt as if we were leaving a precious part of ourselves behind.